Dolce Handknits

SIMPLE, SOPHISTICATED DESIGNS

Kim Dolce

Martingale®
& COMPANY

DEDICATION

For James; you inspire me.

ACKNOWLEDGMENTS

My warmest regards and appreciation to the lovely people I have had the pleasure of working with at Martingale & Company, especially during my all-too-brief visit to Woodinville, Washington. Special thanks to Karen Soltys for your calming manner, to Shelly Garrison for listening so thoughtfully to my ideas, and to Brent Kane for your keen eye behind the camera.

I'd also like to thank Jodi Lewanda, Judy Seip, and Donna Warnell— wonderful knitters all. Without your nimble fingers, I would still be knitting these sweaters. And special thanks to the yarn companies who generously support Dolce Handknits with such beautiful yarns. It was truly a pleasure to work with each and every one of you.

Dolce Handknits: Simple, Sophisticated Designs
© 2010 by Kim Dolce

Martingale & Company®
19021 120th Ave. NE, Suite 102
Bothell, WA 98011 USA
www.martingale-pub.com

Printed in China

15 14 13 12 11 10   8 7 6 5 4 3 2 1

Credits

President & CEO — Tom Wierzbicki

Editor in Chief — Mary V. Green

Managing Editor — Tina Cook

Developmental & Technical Editor — Karen Costello Soltys

Copy Editor — Marcy Heffernan

Design Director — Stan Green

Production Manager — Regina Girard

Illustrator — Laurel Strand

Cover & Text Designer — Shelly Garrison

Photographer — Brent Kane

Mission Statement

Dedicated to providing quality products and service to inspire creativity.

Library of Congress Cataloging-in-Publication Data is available upon request.

ISBN: 978-1-60468-013-3

Contents

Introduction

I was always drawn to the creative process, but never considered myself to be truly creative. That was an elusive thing reserved for those who use color with wild abandon or see wondrous creations in what I see only as someone else's cast-offs. I was always too critical of my own end result to color outside the lines. While I still marvel at the imagination and free spirit of others, I've come to understand that I, too, am creative. Knitting allows me to express both my practical and creative sides so that coloring within the lines is more than acceptable.

Knitting can be as simple or as complex as I choose to make it. I can create something useful and make it something lovely. And most of all, I've chosen knitting as my craft because it's forgiving. With one tug of a string I get to erase my mistakes, learn from them, and try again.

In this, my first book, you'll find designs for every season and many occasions. Most often, I design and knit what I want to wear. As knitters, we put so much time and effort into what we create, I believe it should be something we love and will ultimately wear. I hope you'll find something to love and wear in the designs I've imagined for my own closet.

Yarn Considerations

Knitting, like most things in life, is full of joy and frustration. One of my greatest joys in knitting is finding the perfect yarn for a project. Before I began designing, I remember the frustration of not being able to find the yarn called for in a pattern and my fear of making an uninformed choice when substituting yarn.

In an ideal world, you'd love my yarn selections and be able to find them locally. However, most yarns aren't available indefinitely—or you may simply want to use something different. Yarn substitution is not an exact science, and some of your choices may be better than others—I've found that to be true—but with a little homework, you can increase your chances for success when substituting yarns.

Search out the original yarn, even if you have no intention of using it. The more you know about it—its composition, weight, drape, twist, and hand—the more you'll know what else will work successfully. For each yarn used in this book, I've provided the basic information given on the yarn label as a guide. Local yarn-shop owners and employees have a wealth of knowledge, so shop locally to take advantage of that experience. When it's not possible to visit a yarn shop, try the yarn company's website, Ravelry, or sites like Knitter's Review and Yarndex to research yarn.

While an accurate gauge is essential to achieve the correct size, it's not the be-all and end-all of yarn substitution. Not every yarn with a suggested gauge matching your project will be an appropriate substitute. Remember, a suggested gauge is just that, a suggestion. Most yarns work up beautifully across a small range of needle sizes and gauges. If you fall in love with a yarn, invest in one skein and swatch it on several different needle sizes. Just don't fall in love so deeply that you force a yarn to do what it really doesn't want to do; there will always be another project perfect for that yarn. Be mindful that the fabric you create is not too dense or too loose at the desired gauge. And always swatch a yarn to determine the gauge and suitability of a substitute yarn.

Fiber content is also an important factor in yarn selection. Using a yarn with the same fiber content as the specified yarn will most likely make for a more successful substitution, but it isn't always essential. Knowing something about the properties of a particular fiber will help guide you in selecting a yarn. Elasticity, drape, and weight are all important and should be considered relative to the ultimate use of the garment you plan to knit. If you're unfamiliar with the properties of fibers, there are wonderful books available to guide you. See the list of references in the bibliography on page 95.

Size Considerations

Once you know what you want to knit and have found the perfect yarn, you'll need to decide on a size. For each project in this book, you'll find two sets of measurements—the finished measurements listed at the beginning of each pattern and those in the schematics. Finished measurements give the bust and length of the sweater after it's blocked, seamed, and finished, while the schematic typically gives the measurements of each knitted piece before blocking.

I don't include size designations such as Small, Medium, and Large because with no point of reference, they aren't of much help. As a knitter, you should know your measurements and how you like your clothes to fit, or in other words, the amount of ease you prefer. I give a suggested ease for each sweater, though it's only a suggestion. To determine which size to knit, add the desired ease to your bust measurement, and then select the closest size listed in the finished measurements.

In addition to your bust size, it's helpful to know what length looks best on you. Designs can be adjusted for length, although those without waist shaping are much simpler to alter.

Winter

Portofina

Start the new year dressed to the nines in this off-the-shoulder top with fully fashioned shaping at the waist. For a more casual evening, pair this sexy little top with jeans and heels.

Skill Level

Intermediate

Finished Size

Bust: 27¼ (29½, 31¼, 33¼, 35, 37)"

Length: 17 (17½, 18, 18½, 19, 19½)" to shoulder

Allow 3" to 4" of negative ease for body-hugging fit.

Yarn

450 (485, 510, 575, 635, 700) yds of smooth worsted-weight yarn.

This look is shown in *Zara Plus* from Tahki-Stacy Charles (100% wool; 77 yds/70 m; 50 g) in color 445: 6 (7, 7, 8, 9, 10) balls.

Gauge

19 sts and 28 rnds = 4" over *St st* with smaller needles

Needles

Size 6 and 7 (4mm and 4.5mm) 24" circular needles, or sizes needed to obtain gauge (Short straight needles may be desired for sleeves.)

Notions

Stitch markers, stitch holders, tapestry needle

STITCH GUIDE

Vine Lace (multiple of 9 sts + 1)

Rnd 1: K1, *YO, K2, ssk, K2tog, K2, YO, K1*.

Rnd 2: Knit.

Rnd 3: *YO, K2, ssk, K2tog, K2, YO, K1*, K1.

Rnd 4: Knit.

PATTERN NOTES

This body-hugging sweater needs a yarn with lots of stretch and a fiber with memory like the wonderfully soft (and washable) wool I've chosen. If you live in a warmer clime, a cotton or blend with a touch of Lycra will work nicely too.

See "Techniques" on page 91 for help with make one right (M1R) and make one left (M1L).

BODY

With larger needles, CO 127 (136, 145, 154, 163, 172) sts, PM for beg of rnd and join, taking care not to twist sts on needle. *Knit 1 rnd, purl 1 rnd; rep from * once more. Knit 2 rnds.

Work Rnds 1–4 of *vine lace* twice. Change to smaller needles and work in *St st* (knit every rnd) as foll: If working a size with an even number of sts, knit first rnd, placing a new marker so that an equal number of sts are between each marker. If working a size with an odd number of sts, beg first rnd, K2tog, knit to end of rnd, PM as above—63 (68, 72, 77, 81, 86) sts between markers.

Waist Shaping

Beg with next rnd, dec as foll: *Sl marker, K1, K2tog, work to 2 sts before next marker, ssk, sl marker, K1, K2tog, knit to last 2 sts, ssk. Rep from * around on every 3rd rnd 5 times more—102 (112, 120, 130, 138, 148) sts. Cont without further shaping for 2½ (2½, 2¾, 2¾, 3, 3)". Next rnd, inc as foll: *Sl marker, K1, M1R, work to marker, M1L, sl marker, K1, M1R, knit to end, M1L. Rep from * every 3rd rnd 6 times more—130 (140, 148, 158, 166, 176) sts. Cont even until body meas 13½ (14, 14½, 15, 15½, 16)" from beg.

Separate for Armholes

Beg next rnd, BO 2 (2, 3, 3, 4, 4) sts, work to 2 (2, 3, 3, 4, 4) sts before next marker, BO 4 (4, 6, 6, 8, 8) sts, work to end. Sl next 61 (66, 68, 73, 75, 80) sts to holder for front. Turn and BO 2 (2, 3, 3, 4, 4) sts, then purl to end—61 (66, 68, 73, 75, 80) sts for back.

Working back and forth in *St st* (knit on RS rows, purl on WS rows), work 2 rows even, ending with a WS row.

Armhole Shaping—Back

*Next row (RS), knit to last 4 sts, ssk, K2. Next row (WS), purl to last 4 sts, P2tog, P2. Work 2 rows even. Rep from * 4 times more—51 (56, 58, 63, 65, 70) sts. Place rem sts on holder.

Armhole Shaping—Front

Sl sts for front from holder to smaller needles ready to work a WS row. Join new yarn and work 3 rows even in *St st*. Beg with next row (RS), work armhole shaping as for back—51 (56, 58, 63, 65, 70) sts. Place rem sts on holder.

SLEEVES

With larger needles CO 44 (44, 46, 46, 57, 57) sts. Knit 2 rows. BO 2 (2, 3, 3, 4, 4) sts beg next 2 rows—40 (40, 40, 40, 49, 49) sts.

Work *vine lace* as foll:

Row 1: K3, *YO, K2, ssk, K2tog, K2, YO, K1; rep from * 4 (4, 4, 4, 5, 5) times, K1.

Row 2: Purl.

Row 3: K2, *YO, K2, ssk, K2tog, K2, YO, K1; rep from * 4 (4, 4, 4, 5, 5) times, K2.

Row 4: Purl.

Change to smaller needles and work 2 rows even in *St st*.

Sleeve Shaping

*Next row (RS), knit to last 4 sts, ssk, K2. Next row (WS), purl to last 4 sts, P2tog, P2. Work 6 rows even. Rep from * once more. Then rep 2 dec rows once more—34 (34, 34, 34, 43, 43) sts. Work 1 row even. Place sts on holder.

FINISHING

With RS facing and beg at back left shoulder seam, sl sts from holders to smaller circular needles—170 (180, 184, 194, 216, 226) sts. Join new yarn, PM to mark beg of rnd, join and knit 1 rnd, dec as foll: K2 (0, 0, 2, 0, 2), *K2tog, K2; rep from * around—128 (135, 138, 146, 162, 170) sts. Purl 1 rnd. Knit 1 rnd. Next rnd, BO all sts kwise.

Sew armhole and underarm seams. Weave in ends.

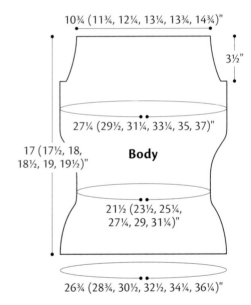

10¾ (11¾, 12¼, 13¼, 13¾, 14¾)"

3½"

27¼ (29½, 31¼, 33¼, 35, 37)"

17 (17½, 18, 18½, 19, 19½)"

Body

21½ (23½, 25¼, 27¼, 29, 31¼)"

26¾ (28¾, 30½, 32½, 34¼, 36¼)"

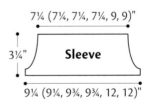

7¼ (7¼, 7¼, 7¼, 9, 9)"

3¼"

Sleeve

9¼ (9¼, 9¾, 9¾, 12, 12)"

PORTOFINO

Point Reyes

How often do you get to say sexy and bulky in
the same sentence? Even a beginning knitter
can be the ultimate snow bunny in this
easy-to-knit après-ski look.

Skill Level

Beginner/Easy

Finished Measurements

Bust: 34 (36, 38, 40, 42, 44, 46)"

Length: 20 (20½, 21¼, 21¾, 21¾, 23, 23½)" (approx,
includes height of turned collar)

Allow about 2" of ease for a standard fit.

Yarn

420 (450, 470, 515, 535, 580, 610) yds smooth super-bulky
yarn.

This look is shown in Blue Sky Alpacas *Bulky* (50%
alpaca, 50% wool; 45 yds/41 m; 100 g) in color 1012 Light
Blue: 10 (10, 11, 12, 12, 13, 14) skeins.

Gauge

8 sts and 12 rnds = 4" over *St st*

Needles

Size 17 (12mm) 24" or 36" circular needle and size P/15
(10 mm) crochet hook, or size needed to obtain gauge

Notions

Stitch marker, stitch holders, tapestry needle

PATTERN NOTES

Length can easily be adjusted at any point before the
armhole shaping on the body and sleeves.

Accurate row gauge is important as the raglan shaping
instructions are written for a set number of rows.

It's more accurate to measure the length of heavy pieces
while they're hanging freely, rather than when lying flat.

See "Techniques" on page 91 for help with half-stitch
seam allowance.

BODY

CO 68 (72, 76, 80, 84, 88, 92) sts; PM to indicate beg of
rnd, join, taking care not to twist sts on needle, and work
in *St st* (knit every rnd) for 14½ (15, 15, 15½, 15 ½, 16,
16½)" or to desired length.

Separate for Armholes

Next rnd, remove marker, BO 6 (8, 8, 10, 10, 12, 12) sts,
knit until there are 28 (28, 30, 30, 32, 32, 34) sts on right-
hand needle for back, BO 6 (8, 8, 10, 10, 12, 12) sts, and
then knit to end of rnd. Sl first set of sts worked to holder
for back, then working back and forth on rem 28 (28, 30,
30, 32, 32, 34) sts for front, turn, and purl 1 WS row.

Raglan Armhole Shaping—Front

Cont in *St st* (knit on RS rows, purl on WS rows) and beg with next row (RS), dec 1 st at each edge as foll: K1, ssk, knit to last 3 sts, K2tog, K1. Rep this dec row every RS row 4 (4, 3, 3, 3, 2, 2) times more, then every 4th row 0 (0, 1, 1, 1, 2, 2) times, ending with a WS row—18 (18, 20, 20, 22, 22, 24) sts. Place rem sts on holder.

Raglan Armhole Shaping—Back

Sl sts held for back to needle ready to work a WS row. Join new yarn and purl 1 row. Beg with next row (RS), work armhole shaping as for front—18 (18, 20, 20, 22, 22, 24) sts. Place rem sts on holder.

SLEEVES

CO 22 (23, 24, 25, 26, 27, 28) sts. Do not join into round. Work back and forth in *St st* for 13½". Next row (RS), inc 1 st at each edge as foll: K1, K1f&b, knit to last 2 sts, K1f&b, K1—24 (25, 26, 27, 28, 29, 30) sts. Work even until sleeve meas 18½" or to desired length to underarm, ending with a WS row.

Raglan Shaping

BO 3 (4, 4, 5, 5, 6, 6) sts beg next 2 rows—18 (17, 18, 17, 18, 17, 18) sts. Beg with next row (RS), dec 1 st at each edge as foll: K1, ssk, knit to last 3 sts, K2tog, K1. Rep this dec row every RS row 4 (4, 3, 1, 1, 0, 0) times more, then every 4th row 0 (0, 1, 2, 2, 3, 3) times, ending with a WS row—8 (7, 8, 9, 10, 9, 10) sts. Place rem sts on holder.

FINISHING

Weave in ends. Block pieces. Sew sleeves to body along armhole edges; then sew underarm seams. Sew seams using a half-stitch seam allowance to reduce bulk.

With RS facing and beg at back left armhole seam, sl sts from holders to needles—52 (50, 56, 58, 64, 62, 68) sts. Join new yarn, PM to indicate beg of rnd, and knit 1 rnd, inc 10 sts evenly around—62 (60, 66, 68, 74, 72, 78) sts. Work K1, P1 rib every rnd until collar meas 7". Next rnd, BO all sts very loosely in patt.

With crochet hook and RS facing, work 1 rnd *sc* around bottom edge of body. Weave in rem ends.

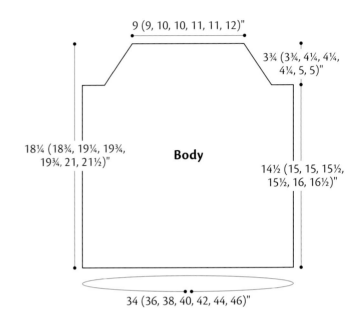

9 (9, 10, 10, 11, 11, 12)"

3¾ (3¾, 4¼, 4¼, 4¼, 5, 5)"

18¼ (18¾, 19¼, 19¾, 19¾, 21, 21½)"

Body

14½ (15, 15, 15½, 15½, 16, 16½)"

34 (36, 38, 40, 42, 44, 46)"

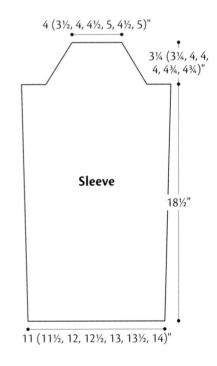

4 (3½, 4, 4½, 5, 4½, 5)"

3¼ (3¼, 4, 4, 4, 4¾, 4¾)"

Sleeve

18½"

11 (11½, 12, 12½, 13, 13½, 14)"

Kilimanjaro

This sweater is the happy marriage of my
inner tomboy with my girlier side. It's my answer
to bundling up against the cold without having
to forsake pretty things.

Skill Level

Intermediate

Finished Measurements

Bust: 37½ (42, 46½)"

Length: 21 (22, 23)"

Allow about 4" of ease for a loose fit.

Yarn

Heavy worsted-weight yarn in 3 colors. A: dark brown 15
(25, 35) yds, B: brown 25 (35, 55) yds, C: tan 800 (1050,
1250) yds.

This look is shown in *Sulka* from Mirasol Yarn (60%
merino wool, 20% alpaca, 20% silk; 55 yds/50 m; 50 g).

A: 204 Cocoa, 1 skein

B: 219 Mocha, 1 skein

C: 207 Caramel, 15 (19, 23) skeins ⑤

Gauge

16 sts and 18 rows = 4" over *vine lace* on smaller needles;
16 sts and 20 rows = 4" over *St st* on size 10 needles

Needles

Size 10 and 11 (6 and 6.5mm) needles and 16" circular in
smaller size for neck, or sizes needed to obtain gauge

Notions

Stitch holders, tapestry needle

STITCH GUIDE

Vine Lace (multiple of 9 sts + 4)

Row 1 (RS): K3, *YO, K2, ssk, K2tog, K2, YO, K1; rep
from * 8 (9, 10) times, K1.

Row 2: Purl.

Row 3: K2, *YO, K2, ssk, K2tog, K2, YO, K1; rep from *
8 (9, 10) times, K2.

Row 4: Purl.

Repeat rows 1–4 for pattern.

Picot BO

BO 2 sts, *sl rem st on right-hand needle back to left-
hand needle, CO 2 sts using backward loop method, BO
4 sts. Rep from * to end.

PATTERN NOTES

Accurate row gauge is important as the raglan shaping
instructions are written for a set number of rows.

To help stay in pattern while shaping, note that on
pattern row 1, the ssk is worked directly above the ssk
and K2tog of the previous row. On pattern row 3, the
ssk is worked two sts before the ssk and K2tog of the
previous row.

See "Techniques" on page 91 for backward-loop cast on.

BACK

With larger needles and A, CO 76 (85, 94) sts. Change to B and knit 2 rows. Change to smaller needles and C and work in *vine lace* patt until back meas 13½ (14, 14½)" from beg, ending with a WS row.

Raglan Shaping

Note: When shaping, if there are not enough sts to work a YO with its companion decrease, work those sts in *St st* (knit on RS rows, purl on WS rows).

Beg with next row (RS), BO 6 (7, 8) sts at beg of next 2 rows—64 (71, 78) sts. Beg with next row (WS), dec every WS row 4 (6, 8) times as foll: P1, P3tog, purl to last 4 sts, sl next 3 sts kwise 1 at a time to right-hand needle, sl same 3 sts back to left-hand needle, keeping them twisted, P3tog tbl, P1—48 (47, 46) sts. Then dec every WS row 12 (11, 10) times as foll: P1, P2tog, purl to last 3 sts, sl next 2 sts kwise 1 at a time to right-hand needle, sl both sts back to left-hand needle, keeping them twisted, P2tog tbl, P1—24 (25, 26) sts. Place rem sts on holder.

FRONT

Work as for back.

SLEEVES

With larger needles and A, CO 49 sts. Change to B and knit 2 rows. Change to smaller needles and C and work in *vine lace* patt until sleeve meas 9" from beg, ending with a WS row.

Sleeve Shaping

Beg with next row (RS), inc 1 st at each edge every 6th row 2 (3, 4) times, working new sts in *St st*—53 (55, 57) sts. Cont in patt as set without further shaping until sleeve meas 18½" from beg, ending with a WS row.

Raglan Shaping

BO 6 (7, 8) sts at beg of next 2 rows—41 sts. Work 1 row even; then beg with next row (WS), dec every WS row 3 times as foll: P1, P3tog, purl to last 4 sts, sl next 3 sts kwise 1 at a time to right-hand needle, sl same 3 sts back to left-hand needle, keeping them twisted, P3tog tbl, P1—29 sts. Then beg dec every WS row 13 times as foll: P1, P2tog, purl to last 3 sts, sl next 2 sts kwise 1 at a time to right-hand needle, sl both sts back to left-hand needle, keeping them twisted, P2tog tbl, P1—3 sts. Work 0 (2, 4) rows even. Place sts on holder.

FINISHING

Weave in ends. Block all pieces. Using a half-stitch seam allowance for all seams, sew sleeves to body along raglan edges. Sew underarm and side seams. With RS facing and beg with sts held for left sleeve, sl sts from holders to 16" circular needle. With C, join and *knit 1 rnd, then purl 1 rnd; rep from * 2 times more. Change to B and knit 1 rnd, purl 1 rnd. Change to A and BO using picot BO. Weave in rem ends.

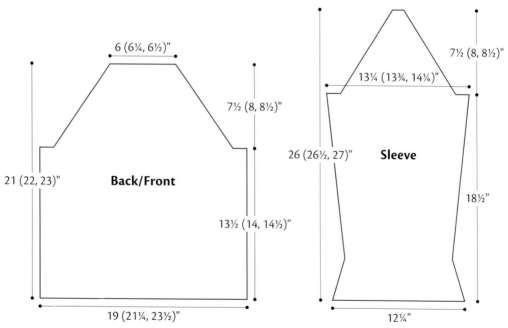

6 (6¼, 6½)"

7½ (8, 8½)"

13¼ (13¾, 14¼)"

7½ (8, 8½)"

26 (26½, 27)" **Sleeve**

21 (22, 23)" **Back/Front**

18½"

13½ (14, 14½)"

19 (21¼, 23½)"

12¼"

Covent Garden

Muted earth tones and a touch of tweed lend a classic feel to this cardigan, while the ruffled hem and collar with picot edging add enough playfulness to keep it from being too staid.

Skill Level
Intermediate/Advanced

Finished Measurements
Bust: 33¾ (35¾, 37¾, 39¾, 41¾)"

Length: 20¾ (21¼, 22¼, 23¼, 24¼)"

Allow about 2" of ease for a standard fit.

Yarn
1125 (1250, 1325, 1450, 1550) yds MC; 75 yds CC; worsted-weight yarn.

This look is shown in *Brae Tweed* from Knit One, Crochet Too (60% merino wool, 20% baby llama, 10% bamboo, 10% Donegal tweed; 109 yds/100 m; 50 g).

MC: 810 Lichen, 11 (12, 13, 14, 15) skeins

CC: 879 Peat, 1 skein for all sizes (4)

Gauge
31 sts and 29 rows = 4" over *baby cable rib* before blocking; 20 sts and 28 rows = 4" over *St st*

Needles
Size 7 (4.5mm) needles and same size 16" circular needle for collar, or size needed to obtain gauge

Notions
Nine ⅝"-diameter buttons, split-ring stitch markers, tapestry needle

STITCH GUIDE

Ruffled Edge

K1, *K2, sl first st over second and off right-hand needle; rep from * to last st, K1.

Baby Cable Rib (multiple of 4 sts + 2)

Rows 1 and 3 (WS): K2, *P2, K2; rep from * to end.

Row 2: P2, *K2, P2; rep from * to end.

Row 4: P2, *RT, P2; rep from * to end.

Rep rows 1–4 for pattern.

RT (Right Twist): K2tog, leaving sts on left-hand needle, insert right-hand needle back into first of 2 sts just knit and knit it again, then slip both sts from left-hand needle together.

Note: When working inc or dec rows, if there are not enough sts to work the RT on row 4, simply knit the rem sts until increasing or decreasing provides enough sts to work the RT.

K2xP2 Rib

Row 1 (WS): P2, *K2, P2; rep from * to end.

Row 2: K2, *P2, K2; rep from * to end.

Rep rows 1 and 2 for pattern.

Picot BO

BO 2 sts, *sl rem st on right-hand needle back to left-hand needle, CO 2 sts using backward-loop method, BO 4 sts; rep from * to end.

PATTERN NOTES

Sweater is shaped at the waist during blocking.

See "Techniques" on page 91 for help with picking up stitches and backward-loop cast on.

BACK

With CC, CO 226 (242, 258, 274, 290) sts, PM every 25 sts to aid counting. Work *ruffled edge*—114 (122, 130, 138, 146) sts. Change to MC and beg with a WS row, work in *baby cable rib* until back meas 12 (12½, 12½, 13, 13½)" from beg, ending with a WS row.

Armhole Shaping

Note: BO sts in patt throughout. When binding off on patt row 4, ignore RT and BO as for *St st*.

BO 7 (8, 9, 9, 9) sts beg of next 2 rows. Beg next row (RS), dec 1 st at each edge every RS row 7 (6, 9, 9, 9) times as foll: Ssk, work in patt to last 2 sts, K2tog—86 (94, 94, 102, 110) sts. Cont in patt as set without further shaping until back meas 20 (20½, 21½, 22½, 23½)" from beg, ending with a WS row. PM to indicate center 38 (42, 44, 44, 48) sts for back neck.

Shoulder and Neck Shaping

Next row (RS), BO 8 (9, 9, 10, 11) sts, cont in patt as set to end. Next row (WS), BO 8 (9, 9, 10, 11) sts, work in patt to first marker, join new yarn and BO 38 (42, 44, 44, 48) sts for back neck, cont in patt as set to end. Work both sides of neck at the same time with separate balls of yarn. Next row (RS), BO 8 (8, 8, 9, 10) sts, cont in patt as set to 2 sts before first neck edge, K2tog. Beg opp neck edge with ssk, cont in patt as set to end. Next row (WS), BO 8 (8, 8, 9, 10) sts, cont in patt to end of opp shoulder. Next row (RS), BO rem 7 (8, 7, 9, 9) sts for first shoulder, work in patt to end. Next row (WS), BO rem 7 (8, 7, 9, 9) sts.

RIGHT FRONT

With CC, CO 114 (122, 130, 138, 146) sts. Work *ruffled edge*—58 (62, 66, 70, 74) sts. Change to MC and beg with a WS row, work in *baby cable rib* until front meas 12 (12½, 12½, 13, 13½)" from beg, ending with a RS row.

Armhole Shaping

Next row (WS), BO 7 (8, 9, 9, 9) sts, cont in patt to end. Beg with next row (RS), dec 1 st at armhole edge every RS row 7 (6, 9, 9, 9) times as foll: work in patt to last 2 sts, K2tog—44 (48, 48, 52, 56) sts. Cont in patt as set without further shaping until front meas 17½ (18, 19, 20, 21)" from beg, ending with a WS row.

Neck Shaping

Next row (RS), BO 5 (5, 5, 5, 6) sts at neck edge, cont in patt to end. Beg next RS row, BO 4 (4, 4, 5, 5) sts. Beg next RS row, BO 3 (4, 4, 4, 4) sts. Beg next RS row, BO 2 (3, 3, 3, 3) sts. Beg with next row (WS), dec 1 st at neck edge every row 4 (4, 5, 6, 7) times as foll: On WS rows, work in patt to last 2 sts, ssp. On RS rows, ssk, work in patt to end. Then dec 1 st at neck edge every RS row 3 (3, 3, 1, 1) times as instructed above—23 (25, 24, 28, 30) sts. Cont in patt as set without further shaping until front meas 20 (20½, 21½, 22½, 23½)" from beg, ending with a RS row.

Shoulder Shaping

Beg next row (WS), BO 8 (9, 9, 10, 11) sts, work in patt to end. Work 1 row even. Beg next row (WS), BO 8 (8, 8, 9, 10) sts, work in patt to end. Next WS row, BO rem 7 (8, 7, 9, 9) sts.

LEFT FRONT

Work as for right front until piece meas 12 (12½, 12½, 13, 13½)" from beg, ending with a WS row.

Armhole Shaping

Beg next row (RS), BO 7 (8, 9, 9, 9) sts, cont in patt to end. Beg with next RS row, dec 1 st at armhole edge every RS row 7 (6, 9, 9, 9) times as foll: ssk, work in patt to end—44 (48, 48, 52, 56) sts. Cont in patt as set without further shaping until front meas 17½ (18, 19, 20, 21)" from beg, ending with a RS row.

Neck Shaping

Next row (WS), BO 5 (5, 5, 5, 6) sts at neck edge, cont in patt to end. Beg next WS row, BO 4 (4, 4, 5, 5) sts. Beg next WS row, BO 3 (4, 4, 4, 4) sts. Beg next WS row, BO 2 (3, 3, 3, 3) sts. Beg next row (RS), dec 1 st at neck edge every row 4 (4, 5, 6, 7) times as foll: On RS rows, work in patt to last 2 sts, K2tog. On WS rows, P2tog, cont in patt to end. Then dec 1 st at neck edge every RS row 3 (3, 3, 1, 1) times as instructed above—23 (25, 24, 28, 30) sts. Cont in patt as set without further shaping until front meas 20 (20½, 21½, 22½, 23½)" from beg, ending with a WS row.

Shoulder Shaping

Beg next row (RS), BO 8 (9, 9, 10, 11) sts, work in patt to end. Beg next RS row, BO 8 (8, 8, 9, 10) sts, work in patt to end. Next RS row, BO rem 7 (6, 7, 9, 9) sts.

SLEEVES

With CC, CO 98 (106, 114, 122, 130) sts. Work *ruffled edge*—50 (54, 58, 62, 66) sts. Change to MC and work row 1 of *baby cable rib*.

Sleeve Shaping

Beg next row (RS), inc 1 st at each edge every 4th row 9 (9, 8, 7, 7) times, then every 6th row 13 (13, 14, 15, 15) times, taking new sts into patt when possible—94 (98, 102, 106, 110) sts. Cont in patt as set without further shaping until sleeve meas 16½ (16½, 16¾, 17, 17)" from beg, ending with a WS row.

Cap Shaping

BO 7 (7, 8, 8, 8) sts beg next 2 rows—80 (84, 86, 90, 94) sts. Dec 1 st at each edge every RS row 7 (8, 9, 10, 12) times as foll: ssk, work in patt to last 2 sts, K2tog—66 (68, 68, 70, 70) sts. Dec 1 st at each edge every row 13 (14, 14, 14, 13) times as foll: On WS rows, P2tog, work in patt to last 2 sts, ssp. On RS rows, ssk, work in patt to last 2 sts, K2tog—40 (40, 40, 42, 44) sts. BO 3 (3, 3, 4, 5) sts beg of next 4 rows. BO rem 28 (28, 28, 26, 24) sts.

FINISHING

Weave in ends. Wet block to finished measurements as shown in schematic on page 24. Sew shoulder seams. Sew sleeves in place. Sew underarm and side seams.

Button Band

With RS facing and MC, pick up 3 sts for every 4 rows along left front from beg of neck shaping to bottom edge. Knit 2 rows. Next row, BO kwise using *picot BO*.

Buttonhole Band

PM for buttonholes on right front ½" below point where neck shaping beg, ½" above bottom edge, and 7 additional markers evenly spaced between first 2 markers. With RS facing and MC, pick up 3 sts for every 4 rows along right front from bottom edge to beg of neck shaping.

Row 1 (WS): *Knit to marker, YO twice, K2tog; rep from * for rem buttonholes, knit to end.

Row 2: Knit, dropping first YO and knitting second YO.

Row 3: BO kwise using *picot BO*.

Sew buttons to button band.

Collar

With circular needle and WS facing, use MC to pick up 110 (114, 118, 122, 126) sts around neck. Work in *K2xP2 rib* for 3 rows making sure a K2 begs and ends RS rows. Beg with next row (RS), inc 1 st at each edge every RS row 5 (5, 5, 6, 6) times taking new sts into patt—120 (124, 128, 134, 138) sts. Work in patt as set without further shaping for 7 rows. Beg with next RS row, dec 1 st each edge every row 6 (6, 6, 7, 7) times, ending with a WS row—108 (112, 116, 120, 124) sts. Turn work and with RS facing, use working yarn to pick up approx 20 (20, 20, 22, 22) sts along edge from point of collar to neck edge. *Do not* work across sts. Along opp collar edge, join new length of MC and pick up an equal number of sts with opp end of circular needle from point of collar to neck edge. With CC and WS facing (underside of collar), BO all sts kwise using *picot BO*. Weave in rem ends.

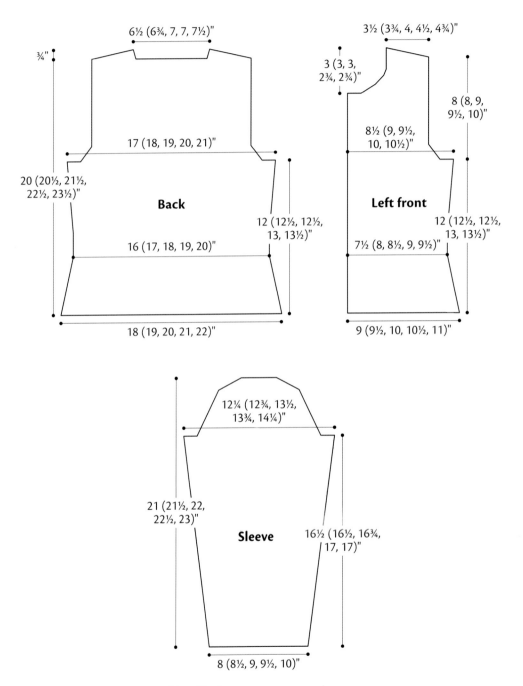

6½ (6¾, 7, 7, 7½)"

¾"

3½ (3¾, 4, 4½, 4¾)"

3 (3, 3, 2¾, 2¾)"

8 (8, 9, 9½, 10)"

17 (18, 19, 20, 21)"

8½ (9, 9½, 10, 10½)"

20 (20½, 21½, 22½, 23½)"

Back

Left front

12 (12½, 12½, 13, 13½)"

12 (12½, 12½, 13, 13½)"

7½ (8, 8½, 9, 9½)"

16 (17, 18, 19, 20)"

18 (19, 20, 21, 22)"

9 (9½, 10, 10½, 11)"

12¼ (12¾, 13½, 13¾, 14¼)"

21 (21½, 22, 22½, 23)"

Sleeve

16½ (16½, 16¾, 17, 17)"

8 (8½, 9, 9½, 10)"

Note: Block to measurements above.

COVENT GARDEN

Spring

Charleston

Adding a separate lace panel to the hem of this cardigan was a simple way to satisfy my love of lace without having to work too hard.

Skill Level

Intermediate

Finished Measurements

Bust: 31 (35, 38¼, 42, 45¼, 49¼)"

Length: 16½ (17, 17½, 18, 18½, 19)"

Allow 1" to 2" of ease for a close fit.

Yarn

770 (825, 955, 1050, 1185, 1275) yds smooth, sport-weight yarn.

This look is shown in *Skinny Cotton* from Blue Sky Alpacas (100% organically grown cotton; 150 yds/137 m; 65 g) in color 304 Zinc: 6 (6, 7, 7, 8, 9) skeins. ③

Gauge

22 sts and 30 rows = 4" over *wildflower knot* pattern; 23 sts and 30 rows = 4" over *St st*

Needles

Size 6 (4.0mm) needles and size E/4 (3.5mm) crochet hook, or size needed to obtain gauge

Notions

Tapestry needle, seven ⅜"-diameter shank-style buttons, stitch holder

STITCH GUIDE

Wildflower Knot (multiple 10 sts + 7)

Row 1 (RS): K7, *P3tog, leaving sts on left-hand needle, YO, then purl same 3 sts tog again, K7; rep from * to end.

Rows 2–8: Purl WS rows, knit RS rows.

Row 9: K2, *P3tog, leaving sts on left-hand needle, YO, then purl same 3 sts tog again, K7*, end last rep K2.

Rows 10–16: Purl WS rows, knit RS rows.

Repeat Rows 1–16 for pattern.

Note: When shaping garment while working *wildflower knot* patt, work the 3 sts of the knot pattern only if they are at least 2 sts from an edge. Otherwise, work rem sts in *St st*.

Vandyke Medallion Edging

Charted pattern appears on page 32.

Row 1 (WS): K2tog, K1, YO, K2tog, K5, K2tog, YO, K2tog, K9, YO, K2tog, K1. (24 sts)

Row 2: Sl 1, K2, YO, K2tog, K1, K2tog, (YO, K2tog) twice, K2, YO, K2tog, K3, K2tog, YO, K3. (23 sts)

Row 3: YO, K4, YO, K2tog, K1, K2tog, YO, K11, YO, K2tog, K1. (24 sts)

Row 4: Sl 1, K2, YO, K2tog, K3, (YO, K2tog) twice, K3, YO, SK2P, YO, K6. (24 sts)

Row 5: YO, K1, K2tog, (YO) twice, K18, YO, K2tog, K1. (26 sts)

Row 6: Sl 1, K2, YO, K2tog, K4, (YO, K2tog) twice, K8, (K1, P1) into double YO, K3. (26 sts)

Row 7: K1, K2tog, (YO) twice, K2tog, (YO) twice, K2tog, K16, YO, K2tog, K1. (27 sts)

Row 8: Sl 1, K2, YO, K2tog, K5, (YO, K2tog) twice, K6, (K1, P1) into double YO, K1, (K1, P1) into double YO, K2. (27 sts)

Row 9: K2tog, K1, K2tog, (YO) twice, K2tog, K3, YO, K1, YO, K2tog, K11, YO, K2tog, K1. (27 sts)

Row 10: Sl 1, K2, YO, K2tog, K3, K2tog, YO, K2tog, (YO, K3) twice, YO, K2tog, K2, (K1, P1) into double YO, K2tog, K1. (27 sts)

Row 11: K2tog, K3, K2tog, YO, K5, YO, K2tog, K10, YO, K2tog, K1. (26 sts)

Row 12: Sl 1, K2, YO, K2tog, K2, (K2tog, YO) twice, K3, YO, K7, YO, K2tog, K1, K2tog. (26 sts)

Repeat rows 1–12 for pattern.

PATTERN NOTES

To decrease on alternate (alt) second and fourth rows for front neck shaping, work the first decrease row as instructed, work one row even, then decrease on next (second) row. Work three rows even, then decrease on next (fourth) row. Continue in this manner, decreasing on alternate second and fourth rows.

See "Techniques" on page 91 for the help with crochet basics.

BACK

CO 87 (97, 107, 117, 127, 137) sts. Beg with a RS row, work in *St st* (knit on RS rows, purl WS rows) for 4 rows. On next row (RS), beg *wildflower knot* patt and work until back meas 4 (4, 4¼, 4½, 4¾, 5)" from beg, ending with a WS row.

Armhole Shaping

BO 3 (4, 6, 8, 10, 11) sts beg next 2 rows. Dec for armholes as foll: Next row (RS), K1, ssk, work in patt to end. Next row (WS), P1, P2tog, purl to end. Rep these 2 dec rows 1 (3, 4, 5, 6, 8) time more—77 (81, 85, 89, 93, 97) sts. Cont even until back meas 11½ (12, 12½, 13, 13½, 14)" from beg, ending with closest WS patt row 4, 6, 12, or 14. BO all sts on next RS row.

RIGHT FRONT

CO 44 (50, 54, 59, 63, 69) sts. Beg with a RS row, work in St st for 4 rows. On next row (RS), beg *wildflower knot* patt, PM before last 7 (3, 7, 2, 6, 2) sts at seam edge, working these sts in St st for selvage. Work until front meas 2½ (2½, 3, 3, 3½, 3½)" from beg, ending with a WS row.

Neck Shaping

Note: Armhole shaping begs before neck shaping is complete. Read ahead to determine when to beg armhole shaping.

On next row (RS), dec 1 st at neck edge as foll: K1, ssk, cont in patt as set to end. Cont dec 1 st at neck edge on alt 2nd and 4th rows (see "Pattern Notes," at left) until a total of 17 (18, 18, 19, 18, 20) sts have been dec at neck edge. AT THE SAME TIME, when front meas 4 (4, 4¼, 4½, 4¾, 5)", beg armhole shaping on next WS row.

Armhole Shaping

Note: After armhole shaping, all sts will be worked in *wildflower knot* patt as set without previously worked selvage sts.

BO 3 (4, 6, 8, 10, 11) sts at beg of next WS row, work in patt to end. Beg with next WS row, dec 1 st at armhole edge every WS row 2 (4, 5, 6, 7, 9) times as foll: P1, P2tog, purl to end—22 (24, 25, 26, 28, 29) sts rem with all neck and armhole shaping completed. Cont even until front meas 11½ (12, 12½, 13, 13½, 14)" from beg, ending with same WS patt row as for back. BO all sts on next RS row.

LEFT FRONT

CO 44 (50, 54, 59, 63, 69) sts. Beg with a RS row, work in St st for 4 rows. On next row (RS), beg *wildflower knot* patt as foll: Work first 7 (3, 7, 2, 6, 2) sts at seam edge in St st for selvage sts, PM, work rem of row in *wildflower knot* patt. Work until front meas 2½ (2½, 3, 3, 3½, 3½)" from beg, ending with a RS row.

Neck Shaping

Note: Armhole shaping begs before neck shaping is complete. Read ahead to determine when to beg armhole shaping.

On next row (WS), dec 1 st at neck edge as foll: P1, P2tog, purl to end. Dec 1 st at neck edge on alt 2nd and 4th rows (see "Pattern Notes") until a total of 17 (18, 18,

19, 18, 20) neck sts have been dec. AT THE SAME TIME, when front meas 4 (4, 4¼, 4½, 4¾, 5)", beg armhole shaping on next RS row.

Armhole Shaping

Note: After armhole shaping, all sts will be worked in *wildflower knot* patt as set without previously worked selvage sts.

BO 3 (4, 6, 8, 10, 11) sts at beg of next RS row. Beg with next RS row, dec 1 st at armhole edge every RS row 2 (4, 5, 6, 7, 9) times as foll: K1, ssk, cont in patt as set to end—22 (24, 25, 26, 28, 29) sts rem with all neck and armhole shaping completed. Cont even until front meas 11½ (12, 12½, 13, 13½, 14)" from beg, ending with same WS patt row as for back. BO all sts on next RS row.

SLEEVES

CO 51 (53, 53, 55, 57, 59) sts. Beg with a RS row, work in *St st* for 4 rows. On next row (RS), work *wildflower knot* patt keeping 2 (3, 3, 4, 5, 1) sts at each edge as selvage sts in *St st*. Cont in patt as set until sleeve meas 1" from beg, ending with a WS row.

Sleeve Shaping

Note: Take all new sts, including those previously worked as selvage sts, into patt as it becomes possible.

Beg with next row (RS), inc 1 st at each edge every 4th row 0 (0, 0, 3, 3, 3) times, then every 6th row 9 (10, 11, 9, 9, 9) times as foll: K1, K1f&b, work in patt to last 2 sts, K1f&b, K1—69 (73, 75, 79, 81, 83) sts. Work even in patt until sleeve meas 11 (11, 11, 11, 11¼, 11¼)" from beg, ending with a WS row.

Cap Shaping

BO 3 (4, 6, 8, 10, 11) sts beg next 2 rows. Next row (RS), K1, ssk, work in patt as set to end. Next row (WS), P1, P2tog, purl to end. Rep 2 dec rows 13 (14, 15, 16, 17, 18) times more—35 (35, 31, 29, 25, 23) sts. BO 5 (5, 4, 4, 3, 2) sts beg next 2 rows. BO 4 (4, 3, 3, 2, 2) sts beg next 2 rows. BO rem 17 (17, 17, 15, 15, 15) sts.

FINISHING

Weave in ends. Block all pieces. Sew shoulder seams. Sew sleeves to body. Sew underarm and side seams.

Lace Panel

CO 26 sts, knit 1 row. Work rows 1–12 of *Vandyke medallion edging* until length of lace panel matches width of sweater from right-front edge around back to left-front edge. When desired length is reached, BO on closest patt row 12. Block, if desired, to meas on schematic (page 32). With crochet hook, work 1 row *sc* across long, straight edge of lace panel so that approx 170 (195, 210, 230, 255, 270) sts are worked. Seam or crochet lace panel to hem edge of body along *sc* edge, easing in as needed.

Picot Edging

With crochet hook and RS facing, beg at right-front hem edge and work 1 row *sc* along right-front edge, around neck and down left front to hem edge, ch 1 and turn. Work back in picot edging as foll: sc 2, *ch 3, sc in same st, skip 1 sc, sc 5; rep from * to point on right front where neck shaping beg, then work button loops by working ch 5 instead of ch 3 for each picot. Sl st into last sc. Fasten off. With crochet hook and RS facing, work 1 rnd *sc* around hem edge of each sleeve. Then work 1 rnd picot edging. Sl st into last sc. Fasten off. Sew buttons to left-front edge opp button loops. Weave in rem ends.

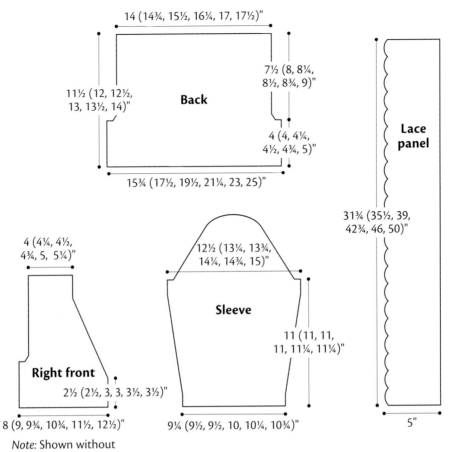

14 (14¾, 15½, 16¼, 17, 17½)"

Back

11½ (12, 12½, 13, 13½, 14)"

7½ (8, 8¼, 8½, 8¾, 9)"

4 (4, 4¼, 4½, 4¾, 5)"

15¾ (17½, 19½, 21¼, 23, 25)"

Lace panel

31¾ (35½, 39, 42¾, 46, 50)"

5"

4 (4¼, 4½, 4¾, 5, 5¼)"

12½ (13¼, 13¾, 14¼, 14¾, 15)"

Sleeve

Right front

2½ (2½, 3, 3, 3½, 3½)"

11 (11, 11, 11, 11¼, 11¼)"

8 (9, 9¾, 10¾, 11½, 12½)"

9¼ (9½, 9½, 10, 10¼, 10¾)"

Note: Shown without lace panel at hem edge.

Vandyke Medallion Edging

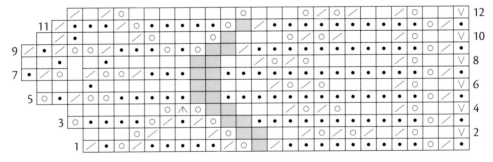

Key

☐	K on RS	╱	K2tog
•	K on WS	∧	SK2P
V	sl	▨	No stitch
○	YO		

Note: Chart begins on WS row, reading row 1 from left to right.

CHARLESTON

Santa Fe

You can't get much simpler than this tunic. The yarn adds texture, and I've added a bit of interest by using exposed seams, adding a rolled neck edge, and leaving side vents at the hem.

Skill Level

Beginner/Easy

Finished Measurements

Bust: 35¼ (37½, 40, 42½, 44¾, 47¼)"

Length: 24 (24½, 25, 25½, 26, 26½)"

Allow 4" to 5" of ease for a loose to oversized fit.

Yarn

1400 (1470, 1600, 1675, 1785, 1875) yds lightly textured sport-weight yarn.

This look is shown in *A-5 1/5 Kusaki-zome* from Habu Textiles (100% silk; 155 yds/140 m; 1 oz) in color 32 Mirobalan: 10 (10, 11, 11, 12, 13) balls.

Gauge

20 sts and 38 rows = 4" over *garter st*

Needles

Size 6 (4mm) needles for sweater and same size 16" circular needle for neck, or size needed to obtain gauge

Notions

Tapestry needle, stitch markers, 2 skeins embroidery floss in matching color for seaming textured yarn

PATTERN NOTES

This sport-weight yarn can be worked effectively on larger needles than called for because of its texture. The resulting fabric is very slinky, so keep a close eye on gauge and length. It's helpful to measure the length of pieces when they're hanging freely.

See "Techniques" on page 91 for help with picking up stitches and whipstitching.

BACK

Loosely CO 90 (96, 102, 108, 114, 120) sts. Work in *garter st* (knit every row) until back meas 24 (24½, 25, 25½, 26, 26½)" or to desired length. BO all sts loosely.

FRONT

Work as for back until front meas 15 (15, 16, 16, 17, 17)". PM to indicate center 2 sts.

Neck Shaping

On next row, knit to first marker, join new yarn, BO 2 center sts, knit to end. Working both sides of neck at the same time with separate balls of yarn, work 1 row even across both sides of neck. Beg next row, dec 1 st at each neck edge every 4th row 18 (18, 18, 19, 19, 20) times as foll: Knit to 2 sts before first neck edge, K2tog. Beg opp neck edge, ssk, knit to end—26 (29, 32, 34, 37, 39) sts rem for each shoulder. Cont even without further shaping until front meas 24 (24½, 25, 25½, 26, 26½)". BO all sts loosely.

SLEEVES

CO 62 (62, 68, 68, 72, 72) sts. Work in *garter st* until sleeve meas 8½" from beg. Next row, inc 1 st at each edge every 12th row 6 times as foll: K1f&b, knit to last st, K1f&b—74 (74, 80, 80, 84, 84) sts. Cont even until sleeve meas 18" or to desired length. BO all sts loosely.

FINISHING

Weave in ends. Thread tapestry needle with all 6 strands of embroidery floss. With WS of front and back held tog, use a whipstitch to seam shoulders, creating a raised seam. Meas 7½ (7½, 8, 8, 8½, 8½)" from each shoulder seam along front and back armhole edge and PM. Whipstitch sleeves to body between markers. Whipstitch underarm and side seams, leaving 3" vents open at hem edge of each side seam.

Neckband

With circular needle and RS facing, beg at right shoulder seam and pick up approx 1 st for every row and 1 st for every BO st around neck. PM, join, and knit every rnd for 1½". BO loosely. Weave in rem ends.

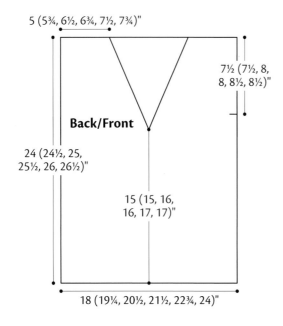

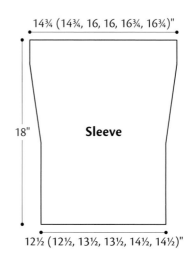

SANTA FE

Ithaca

Fully-fashioned waist shaping and
ever-so-slightly puffed sleeves add a bit of
femininity to this prim and proper tee.

Skill Level

Easy/Intermediate

Finished Measurements

Bust: 31¼ (33¼, 35¼, 37¼, 39¼, 41¼)"

Length: 21 (21½, 22, 22½, 23, 23½)"

Allow 0" of ease for a close fit.

Yarn

755 (830, 920, 1015, 1120, 1235) yds smooth sport-weight yarn

This look is shown in *Ashton* from Plymouth Yarns (50% baby alpaca, 40% fine merino wool, 10% silk; 122 yds; 50 g) in color 1016, Pale Blue: 7 (7, 8, 9, 10, 11) skeins.

Gauge

24 sts and 30 rows = 4" over *St st* with smaller needles

Needles

Sizes 5 and 6 (3.75 mm and 4 mm) needles and smaller size 16" circular needle for neck edging, or sizes needed to obtain gauge

Notions

Tapestry needle, stitch markers

STITCH GUIDE

K2xP1 Rib (multiple of 3 sts + 2)

Row 1 (RS): K2, *P1, K2; rep from * to end.

Row 2: P2, *K1, P2; rep from * to end.

PATTERN NOTES

See "Techniques" on page 91 for help with increases—make one right (M1R), make one left (M1L)—and for picking up stitches.

BACK

With larger needles, CO 98 (104, 110, 116, 122, 128) sts. Work 3 rows *K2xP1 rib*. Change to smaller needles and purl next row (WS), dec 4 sts evenly across row—94 (100, 106, 112, 118, 124) sts. Cont in *St st* (knit on RS, purl on WS) until back meas 1½ (1¾, 2, 2¼, 2½, 2¾)" from beg, ending with a WS row.

Side Shaping

Beg with next row (RS), dec 1 st at each edge every RS row 11 times as foll: K1, ssk, work to last 3 sts, K2tog, K1—72 (78, 84, 90, 96, 102) sts. Work even for 2 (2½, 2¾, 3, 3¼, 3½)". Beg with next RS row, inc 1 st at each edge every RS row 12 times as foll: K1, M1L, knit to last st, M1R, K1—96 (102, 108, 114, 120, 126) sts. Cont even in *St st* until back meas 13½ (13¾, 14, 14¼, 14½, 14¾)" from beg, ending with a WS row.

Armhole Shaping

BO 5 (6, 6, 7, 7, 8) sts beg next 2 rows. Beg with next row (RS), dec 1 st at each edge every RS row 4 (4, 5, 5, 6, 6) times as foll: K1, ssk, work to last 3 sts, K2tog, K1—78 (82, 86, 90, 94, 98) sts. Cont even until back meas 18¾ (19¼, 19¾, 20¼, 20¾, 21¼)" from beg, ending with a WS row. PM to indicate center 38 (40, 42, 44, 46, 48) sts for back neck.

Neck Shaping

On next row (RS), work to first marker, join new yarn, and BO off center 38 (40, 42, 44, 46, 48) sts, knit to end—20 (21, 22, 23, 24, 25) sts rem for each shoulder. Work both sides of neck at the same time with separate balls of yarn. Next row (WS), purl across first neck edge, BO 2 sts beg opp neck edge, purl to end. Next row (RS), knit across first

neck edge, BO 2 sts beg opp neck edge, knit to end. Work 1 row even. Beg with next row (RS), dec 1 st at each neck edge every RS row 3 times as foll: knit to 3 sts before first neck edge, K2tog, K1, beg opp neck edge, K1, ssk, knit to end—15 (16, 17, 18, 19, 20) sts rem for each shoulder. Cont even in *St st* until back meas 20½ (21, 21½, 22, 22½, 23)" from beg, ending with a WS row.

Shoulder Shaping

BO 8 (8, 9, 9, 10, 10) sts for first shoulder, work across to end of opp shoulder. Rep for next row (WS). Next row (RS), BO 7 (8, 8, 9, 9, 10) sts for first shoulder, work across to end of opp shoulder. Rep for next row (WS).

FRONT

Work as for back through armhole shaping. When front meas 15½ (15¾, 16, 16¼, 16½, 16¾)" from beg, PM to indicate center 16 (18, 20, 22, 24, 26) sts for front neck.

Neck Shaping

On next row (RS), work to first marker, join new yarn and BO off center 16 (18, 20, 22, 24, 26) sts, knit to end—31 (32, 33, 34, 35, 36) sts rem for each shoulder. Work both sides of neck at the same time with separate balls of yarn. Next row (WS), purl across first neck edge, BO 3 sts beg opp neck edge, purl to end. Next row (RS), knit across first neck edge, BO 3 sts beg opp neck edge, knit to end. Next row (WS), purl across first neck edge, BO 2 sts beg opp neck edge, purl to end. Next row (RS), knit across first neck edge, BO 2 sts beg opp neck edge, knit to end. Work 1 row even. Beg with next row (RS), dec 1 st at each neck edge every RS row 11 times as foll: knit to 3 sts before first neck edge, K2tog, K1, beg opp neck edge, K1, ssk, knit to end—15 (16, 17, 18, 19, 20) sts rem for each shoulder. Cont even in *St st* until back meas 20½ (21, 21½, 22, 22½, 23)" from beg, ending with a WS row.

Shoulder Shaping

BO 8 (8, 9, 9, 10, 10) sts for first shoulder, work across to end of opp shoulder. Rep for next row (WS). Next row (RS), BO 7 (8, 8, 9, 9, 10) sts for first shoulder, work across to end of opp shoulder. Rep for next row (WS).

SLEEVES

With larger needles, CO 65 (68, 71, 74, 77, 80) sts. Work in *K2xP1 rib* for 3 rows. Change to smaller needles and purl across next row (WS), dec 1 st at each edge—63 (66, 69, 72, 75, 78) sts. Cont in *St st* for 2 rows. Beg with next row (RS), inc 1 st at each edge every RS row 6 times as foll: K1, M1R, work to last st, M1L, K1—75 (78, 81, 84, 87, 90) sts. Cont even in *St st* until sleeve meas 2½" from beg, ending with a WS row.

Cap Shaping

BO 5 (6, 6, 7, 7, 8) sts beg next 2 rows. Beg with next row (RS), dec 1 st at each edge every 4th row 8 times, then every 2nd row 1 (2, 3, 4, 5, 6) time as foll: K1, ssk, work to last 3 sts, K2tog, K1. BO 4 sts beg next 2 rows. On next row (RS), K1 (0, 1, 0, 1, 0), *K2tog; rep from * to end. BO rem 20 (19, 20, 19, 20, 19) sts.

FINISHING

Weave in ends. Block all pieces lightly. Sew shoulder seams. Sew sleeves to body, easing in extra fabric along top of sleeve cap for puffed sleeve. Sew underarm and side seams.

Neckband

With circular needle and RS facing, beg at right shoulder seam along neck edge and pick up approx 3 sts for every 4 rows along vertical edges and 1 st for every BO st along horizontal edges around neck, counting sts and adjusting so that total number of sts is a multiple of 3 sts. Work 2 rnds of *K2xP1 rib* as foll: *K2, P1; rep from * to end. Next rnd, BO in patt. Weave in rem ends.

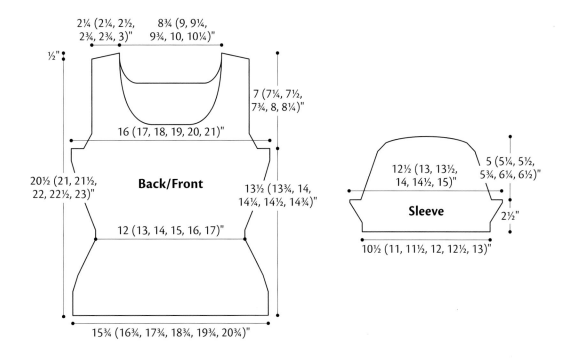

Capri

This flirty little eyelet cardigan is trimmed with knitted flowers that are quicker to make than you might imagine. Work the flowers in one color or many, place them as shown, around the neck only, or cluster a small bunch as a corsage to one side. If you opt for a wool yarn, consider felting the flowers before attaching them.

Skill Level

Easy/Intermediate

Finished Meaurements

Bust: 35 (38, 41¼, 44½, 47¾)"

Length: 18 (19, 20, 21, 22)"

Allow about 2" of ease for a standard fit.

Yarn

970 (1090, 1215, 1360, 1525) yds worsted-weight yarn.

This look is shown in *Cotton Supreme* from Universal Yarn (100% cotton; 180 yds/165 m; 100 g) in color 502, White: 6 (7, 7, 8, 9) skeins. (4)

Gauge

20 sts and 26 rows = 4" over *eyelet stitch*; 21 sts and 26 rows = 4" over *St st*

Needles

Size 7 (4.5 mm) needles and same size 24" circular needle for front bands, or size needed to obtain gauge

Notions

Tapestry needle, split-ring stitch markers, eight ⅝"-diameter buttons

STITCH GUIDE

Eyelet Stitch (multiple of 8 sts)

Row 1 (RS): Knit.

Row 2: Purl.

Row 3: *K6, YO, K2tog; rep from * to end. (For 2nd and 4th sizes only: on front sections, end last rep K4.)

Row 4: Purl.

Row 5: Knit.

Row 6: Purl.

Row 7: K2, *YO, K2tog, K6; rep from * until 6 sts rem, YO, K2tog, K4. (For 2nd and 4th sizes only: on front sections, end last rep YO, K2tog.)

Row 8: Purl.

Repeat rows 1–8 for pattern.

PATTERN NOTES

See "Techniques" on page 91 for help with make one right (M1R), make one left (M1L), and picking up stitches.

BACK

CO 77 (86, 92, 101, 110) sts and work 3 rows *K2xP1 rib* as foll:

Row 1 (RS): K2, *P1, K2; rep from * to end.

Row 2: P2, *K1, P2; rep from * to end.

Row 3: Rep row 1.

Next row (WS), purl, inc 3 (2, 4, 3, 2) sts evenly across row—80 (88, 96, 104, 112) sts. On next row (RS), beg *eyelet st* and work until back meas 1½" from beg. *On next RS row inc 1 st at each edge as foll: K1, M1L, work in patt as set to last st, M1R, K1. Work even in *eyelet st* for 2". Rep from * 3 times more—88 (96, 104, 112, 120) sts. Cont without further shaping until back meas 10 (10½, 11, 11½, 12)" from beg, ending with a WS row.

Armhole Shaping

BO 5 (6, 7, 8, 9) sts beg next 2 rows—78 (84, 90, 96, 102) sts. Beg with next row (RS), dec 1 st at each armhole edge every RS row 5 (6, 7, 8, 9) times as foll: K1, ssk, work in patt as set to last 3 sts, K2tog, K1—68 (72, 76, 80, 84) sts. Cont in patt without further shaping until back meas 17 (18, 19, 20, 21)" from beg, ending with a WS row.

Shoulder Shaping

BO 6 (7, 7, 7, 8) sts beg next 2 rows. BO 6 (6, 7, 7, 7) sts beg next 2 rows. BO 6 (6, 6, 7, 7) sts beg next 2 rows. BO rem 32 (34, 36, 38, 40) sts for back neck.

RIGHT FRONT

CO 39 (42, 45, 51, 54) sts and work 3 rows *K2xP1 rib* as foll:

Row 1 (RS): K3, *P1, K2; rep from * to end.

Row 2: *P2, K1; rep from * to last 3 sts, P3.

Row 3: Rep row 1.

Purl next row (WS), inc 1 (2, 3, 1, 2) st evenly across row—40 (44, 48, 52, 56) sts. On next row (RS), beg *eyelet st* and work until front meas 1½" from beg. *On next RS row, inc 1 st at side-seam edge as foll: Work in patt as set to last st, M1R, K1. Cont even in *eyelet st* for 2". Rep from * 3 times more—44 (48, 52, 56, 60) sts. Cont without further shaping until front meas 9 (9¾, 10½, 11, 11½)" from beg, ending with a WS row.

Neck Shaping

Note: Armhole shaping begins before neck shaping is complete.

Beg with next row (RS), dec 1 st at neck edge every RS row 10 (11, 12, 13, 14) times, then every 4th row 6 times as foll: K1, ssk, work in patt as set to end. AT THE SAME TIME, when front meas 10 (10½, 11, 11½, 12)" from beg, cont neck shaping and beg armhole shaping on next WS row.

Armhole Shaping

BO 5 (6, 7, 8, 9) sts beg next row (WS). Beg with next row (RS), dec 1 st at armhole edge every RS row 5 (6, 7, 8, 9) times as foll: Work in patt as set to last 3 sts, K2tog, K1. When all neck and armhole shaping is complete, 18 (19, 20, 21, 22) sts rem. Cont in patt without further shaping until front meas 17 (18, 19, 20, 21)" from beg, ending with a RS row.

Shoulder Shaping

BO 6 (7, 7, 7, 8) sts beg next row (WS). Work 1 row even. BO 6 (6, 7, 7, 7) sts beg next WS row. Work 1 row even. BO rem 6 (6, 6, 7, 7) sts.

LEFT FRONT

CO 39 (42, 45, 51, 54) sts and work 3 rows *K2xP1 rib* as foll:

Row 1 (RS): *K2, P1; rep from * to last 3 sts, K3.

Row 2: P3, *K1, P2; rep from * to end.

Row 3: Rep row 1.

Purl next row (WS), inc 1 (2, 3, 1, 2) st evenly across row—40 (44, 48, 52, 56) sts. On next row (RS), beg *eyelet st* and work until front meas 1½" from beg. *On next RS row inc 1 st at side-seam edge as foll: K1, M1L, work in patt as set to end. Cont even in *eyelet st* for 2". Rep from * 3 times more—44 (48, 52, 56, 60) sts. Cont without further shaping until front meas 9 (9¾, 10½, 11, 11½)" from beg, ending with a WS row.

Neck Shaping

Note: Armhole shaping begins before neck shaping is complete.

Beg with next RS row, dec 1 st at neck edge every RS row 10 (11, 12, 13, 14) times, then every 4th row 6 times as foll: Work in patt as set to last 3 sts, K2tog, K1. AT THE SAME TIME, when front meas 10 (10½, 11, 11½, 12)" from beg, cont neck shaping and beg armhole shaping on next RS row.

Armhole Shaping

BO 5 (6, 7, 8, 9) sts beg next row (RS). Beg with next RS row, dec 1 st at armhole edge every RS row 5 (6, 7, 8, 9) times as foll: K1, ssk, work in patt as set to end. When all neck and armhole shaping is complete, 18 (19, 20, 21, 22) sts rem. Cont in patt without further shaping until front meas 17 (18, 19, 20, 21)" from beg, ending with a WS row.

Shoulder Shaping

BO 6 (7, 7, 7, 8) sts beg next row (RS). Work 1 row even. BO 6 (6, 7, 7, 7) sts beg next RS row. Work 1 row even. BO rem 6 (6, 6, 7, 7) sts.

SLEEVES

CO 47 (47, 50, 50, 50) sts and work 3 rows *K2xP1 rib* as foll:

Row 1 (RS): K2, *P1, K2; rep from * to end.

Row 2: P2, *K1, P2; rep from * to end.

Row 3: Rep row 1.

Purl next row (WS), inc 1 (1, 2, 2, 2) st evenly across row—48 (48, 52, 52, 52) sts. On next row (RS), beg *eyelet st* and work until sleeve meas 1" from beg, ending with a WS row.

Sleeve Shaping

Beg with next row (RS), inc 1 st at each edge every 4th row 0 (2, 2, 7, 11) times, then every 6th row 9 (9, 9, 6, 4) times as foll: K1, M1L, work in patt as set to last st, M1R, K1—66 (70, 74, 78, 82) sts. Cont without further shaping until sleeve meas 11½ (11¾, 12, 12¼, 12½)" from beg, ending with a WS row.

Cap Shaping

BO 5 (6, 7, 8, 9) sts beg next 2 rows—56 (58, 60, 62, 64) sts. Beg with next row (RS), dec 1 st at each edge every RS row 16 (17, 18, 19, 20) times as foll: K1, ssk, work in patt as set to last 3 sts, K2tog, K1—24 sts. Beg with next RS row, BO 3 sts beg next 4 rows. BO rem 12 sts.

FINISHING

Weave in ends. Block all pieces. Sew shoulder seams. Sew sleeves in place. Sew underarm and side seams.

Front Band

PM for buttonholes along right-front edge as foll: PM ½" below point where neck shaping beg, PM ½" above bottom edge, then place 6 more markers evenly spaced between first 2 markers. With circular needle and RS facing, pick up approx 3 sts for every 4 rows around entire front from right-front hem edge, across back neck to left-front hem edge, counting sts and adjusting as needed so total number of sts is a multiple of 3 sts plus 2 sts. Turn. Work band as foll:

Row 1 (WS): P2, *K2, P1; rep from * to last st, P1.

Row 2 (buttonhole row): *Work in patt as set to marker, BO 1 st, YO; rep from * for rem buttonholes, cont in *K2xP1 rib* to end.

Row 3 (WS): BO in patt.

Sew buttons to button band opp buttonholes.

Flowers

Make approx 48 (51, 54, 57, 60) flowers as foll: CO 35 sts. *K1, BO next 5 sts* (*Note:* 2 sts on right-hand needle after working 1 rep). Rep between * to end—10 sts rem. Cut yarn, leaving several inches of yarn to thread on tapestry needle and run through rem sts. Secure flowers to cardigan around front edges and back neck with loose yarn ends. Weave in ends.

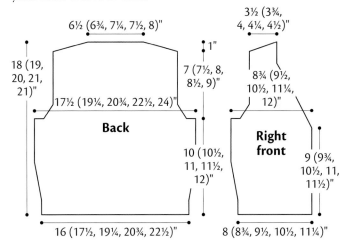

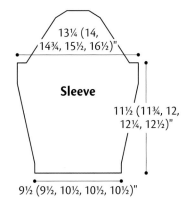

Summer

Chapel Hill

In my mind, this pretty little tank is the perfect summer knit. The fingering-weight hemp is easy to care for, softens beautifully with washing, and is comfortable on even the warmest of days. Not in the mood for summer knits? Imagine it dressed up a bit in lightweight wool with a sleek pencil skirt, or for an evening look use a shimmery or sequined yarn.

Skill Level

Easy/Intermediate

Finished Measurements

Bust: 33½ (35¾, 37¾, 40, 42¼, 44¼, 46½, 48¾)"

Length: 19½ (20¼, 21, 21¾, 22½, 23¼, 24, 24¾)"

Allow about 1" of ease for a close fit.

Yarn

745 (825, 905, 990, 1085, 1185, 1290, 1375) yds smooth fingering-weight yarn.

This look is knit in *allhemp3* from LanaKnits (100% hemp; 165 yds/150 m; 50 g) in color 10 Pearl: 5 (5, 6, 6, 7, 8, 8, 9) skeins. ①

Gauge

33 sts and 38 rows = 4" with smaller needles over *St st*; 29 sts = 4" with larger needles over *vine lace*

Needles

Size 2 and 3 (2.75 and 3.25mm) needles and smaller size 16" circular needle for edging, or sizes needed to obtain gauge

Notions

Stitch markers, tapestry needle, 2 to 2½ yds ½"-wide ribbon

STITCH GUIDE

Vine Lace (multiple of 9 sts + 4)

Row 1 and 3 (WS): Purl.

Row 2: K3, *YO, K2, ssk, K2tog, K2, YO, K1; rep from * to last st, K1.

Row 4: K2, *YO, K2, ssk, K2tog, K2, YO, K1; rep from * to last 2 sts, K2.

Repeat rows 1–4 for pattern.

PATTERN NOTES

See "Techniques" on page 91 for help with picking up stitches.

BACK

With larger needles, CO 130 (139, 148, 157, 166, 175, 184, 193) sts. Work in *garter st* (knit every row) for 4 rows. Next row (WS), beg working *vine lace* patt. Cont in patt until back meas approx 6½ (6¾, 7, 7¼, 7½, 7¾, 8, 8¼)" from beg, ending with a WS row. Change to smaller needles, knit 1 row, inc 10 sts evenly spaced across row—140 (149, 158, 167, 176, 185, 194, 203) sts. Purl 1 row.

Eyelet Row

Work next row (RS) as foll: K2 (4, 4, 3, 3, 2, 4, 3), *YO, K2tog, K3; rep from *, end last rep K1 (3, 2, 2, 1, 1, 3, 3)—28 (29, 31, 33, 35, 37, 38, 40) eyelets made. Cont in *St st* (knit on RS, purl on WS) until back meas 12 (12½, 13, 13½, 14, 14½, 15, 1½)" from beg, ending with a WS row.

Armhole Shaping

BO 10 (10, 10, 10, 11, 11, 12, 12) sts beg of next 2 rows. BO 4 (4, 6, 6, 6, 7, 7, 8) sts beg of next 2 rows. BO 3 (3, 3, 3, 4, 4, 4, 4) sts beg of next 2 rows—106 (115, 120, 129, 134, 141, 148, 155) sts. Beg with next row (RS), dec 1 st at each armhole edge every RS row 8 (10, 10, 10, 10, 10, 11, 11) times as foll: Ssk, knit to last 2 sts, K2tog. Then dec 1 st each edge every 4th row 2 (2, 2, 3, 3, 3, 3, 3) times—86 (91, 96, 103, 108, 115, 120, 127) sts. Cont even in *St st* until back meas 15¾ (16½, 17, 18, 18½, 19, 19¾, 20¼)" from beg, ending with a WS row. PM to indicate center 40 (43, 46, 51, 54, 59, 62, 67) sts for back neck.

Neck Shaping

On next row (RS), work to first marker, join new yarn and BO center 40 (43, 46, 51, 54, 59, 62, 67) sts, knit to end. Work both sides of neck at the same time with separate balls of yarn. Next row (WS), purl across first side of neck, BO 3 sts beg opp neck edge, purl to end. Next row (RS), knit across first side of neck, BO 3 sts beg opp neck edge, knit to end. Next row (WS), purl across first side of neck, BO 2 sts beg opp neck edge, purl to end. Next row (RS), knit across first side of neck, BO 2 sts beg opp neck edge, knit to end. Work 1 row even. *On next row (RS), knit to 2 sts before first neck edge, K2tog, beg opp neck edge ssk, knit to end; rep from * 4 times more—13 (14, 15, 16, 17, 18, 19, 20) sts rem for each strap. Cont even in *St st* until back meas 19½ (20¼, 21, 21¾, 22½, 23¼, 24, 24¾)" from beg, ending with a WS row. BO all sts.

FRONT

Work as for back to armhole shaping, ending with a WS row. PM to indicate center 40 (43, 46, 51, 54, 59, 62, 67) sts for front neck.

Armhole Shaping

Note: Neck shaping begins before armhole shaping is complete. Read ahead to determine when to begin neck shaping.

BO 10 (10, 10, 10, 11, 11, 12, 12) sts beg of next 2 rows. BO 4 (4, 6, 6, 6, 7, 7, 8) sts beg of next 2 rows. BO 3 (3, 3, 3, 4, 4, 4, 4) sts beg of next 2 rows—106 (115, 120, 129, 134, 141, 148, 155) sts. Beg with next row (RS), dec 1 st at each armhole edge every RS row 8 (10, 10, 10, 10, 10, 11, 11) times as foll: ssk, knit to last 2 sts, K2tog. Then dec 1 st each edge every 4th row 2 (2, 2, 3, 3, 3, 3, 3) times. AT THE SAME TIME, when front meas 13 (13½, 14, 14½, 15, 15¼, 15¾, 16¼)", beg neck shaping on next RS row.

Neck Shaping

Next row (RS), work to first marker, join new yarn and BO center 40 (43, 46, 51, 54, 59, 62, 67) sts for front neck. Work both sides of neck at the same time with separate balls of yarn while cont armhole shaping as indicated. Next row (WS), purl across first side of neck, BO 3 sts beg opp neck edge, purl to end. Next row (RS), knit across first side of neck, BO 3 sts beg opp neck edge, knit to end. Next row (WS), purl across first side of neck, BO 2 sts beg opp neck edge, purl to end. Next row (RS), knit across first side of neck, BO 2 sts beg opp neck edge, knit to end. Work 1 row even. *On next row (RS), knit to 2 sts before first neck edge, K2tog, beg opp neck edge ssk, knit to end; rep from * 4 times more—13 (14, 15, 16, 17, 18, 19, 20) sts rem for each strap with armhole and neck shaping complete. Cont even in *St st* until front meas 19½ (20¼, 21, 21¾, 22½, 23¼, 24, 24¾)" from beg, ending with a WS row. BO all sts.

FINISHING

Weave in ends. Block pieces. Sew shoulder and side seams.

With circular needles and RS facing, beg at right underarm seam and pick up 1 st for every BO st and 3 sts for every 4 rows around armhole, PM, and purl 1 rnd. Knit 1 rnd. Next rnd, BO all sts purlwise. Rep for opp armhole edge. With circular needles and RS facing, beg at right shoulder seam and pick up 1 st for every BO st and 3 sts for every 4 rows around neck, PM, and purl 1 rnd. Knit 1 rnd. Next rnd, BO all sts purlwise. Weave in rem ends. Thread silk ribbon through eyelets and tie in a bow. Trim ribbon ends at a 45° angle to prevent fraying.

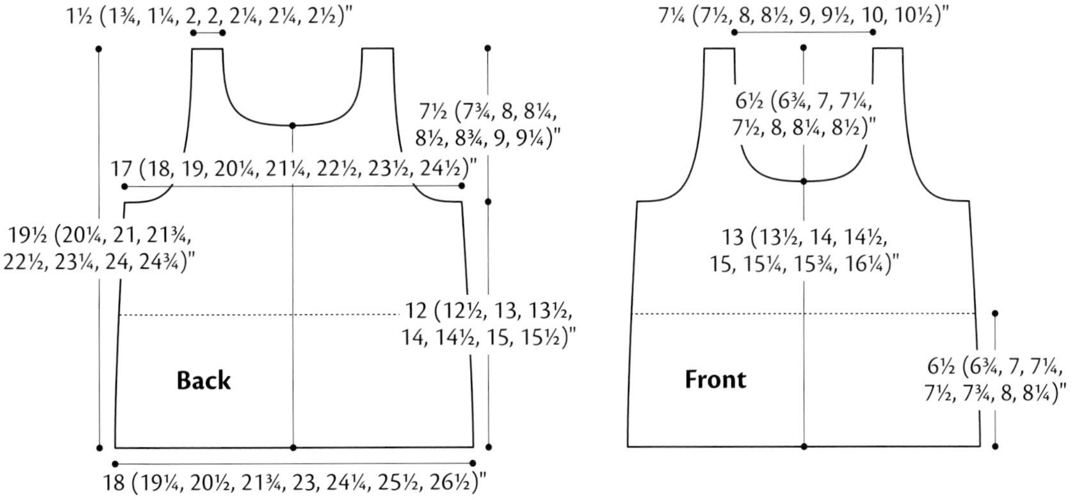

1½ (1¾, 1¼, 2, 2, 2¼, 2¼, 2½)"

7¼ (7½, 8, 8½, 9, 9½, 10, 10½)"

7½ (7¾, 8, 8¼, 8½, 8¾, 9, 9¼)"

6½ (6¾, 7, 7¼, 7½, 8, 8¼, 8½)"

17 (18, 19, 20¼, 21¼, 22½, 23½, 24½)"

19½ (20¼, 21, 21¾, 22½, 23¼, 24, 24¾)"

13 (13½, 14, 14½, 15, 15¼, 15¾, 16¼)"

12 (12½, 13, 13½, 14, 14½, 15, 15½)"

Back

Front

6½ (6¾, 7, 7¼, 7½, 7¾, 8, 8¼)"

18 (19¼, 20½, 21¾, 23, 24¼, 25½, 26½)"

Seville

Depending on the yarn you choose, this lace
bolero is chic enough to top a little black dress,
or you can play it down with jeans and a tiny tee.
I love it somewhere in between—over summery
dresses. The overall lace looks more complex than
it really is and the row-by-row instructions put this
pretty top within reach of beginning lace knitters.

Skill Level

Intermediate

Finished Measurements

Bust: 31½ (35½, 39½)"

Length: 11 (12¾, 14½)"

Allow 0" to negative 2" of ease for a body-hugging fit.

Yarn

650 (800, 950) yds smooth fingering-weight yarn.

This look is knit in *Zoe* from Shalimar Yarns (100%
superwash Australian merino; 450 yds; 100 g) in color,
Merlin's Beard: 2 (2, 3) skeins.

Gauge

24 sts and 36 rows = 4" over *mini leaf stitch* patt after
blocking; 33 sts = 4" over *St st*

Needles

Size 3 (3.25mm) needles and size D/3 (3.25mm) crochet
hook, or size needed to obtain gauge

Notions

Tapestry needle

STITCH GUIDE

Mini Leaf Stitch (multiple of 6 sts + 1)

Row 1 (and all WS rows): Purl.

Row 2: K1, *K2tog, YO, K1, YO, ssk, K1*.

Row 4: K2tog, *YO, K3, YO, sskp*, end last rep ssk.

Row 6: K1, *YO, ssk, K1, K2tog, YO, K1*.

Row 8: K2, *YO, sskp, YO, K3*, end last rep K2.

Rows 1–8 make up one patt set.

Note: When *6-st rep* is used in instructions, work the
6 sts of *mini leaf stitch* patt between * for row indicated in
instructions. Or you can follow the 6-st rep shown in the
mini leaf stitch chart on page 61.

PATTERN NOTES

General shaping instructions are followed by detailed
row-by-row instructions. If following general
instructions, note that when shaping, if there are not
enough stitches to work a yarn over with its companion
decrease, work those stitches in stockinette stitch.

To decrease on alternate second and fourth rows, work the
first decrease row as instructed, work one row even, then
decrease on next (second) row. Work three rows even,
then decrease on next (fourth) row. Continue in this
manner, decreasing on alternate second and fourth rows.

Similarly, to decrease on alternate eighth and tenth rows, work seven rows even before an eighth row decrease and work nine rows even before a tenth-row decrease.

See "Techniques" on page 91 for help with crochet basics.

BACK

CO 91 (103, 115) sts and work the 8 rows of *mini leaf stitch* 4 (5, 6) times—4 (5, 6) patt sets worked. Back meas approx 3½ (4½, 5¼)" from beg.

Armhole Shaping—General

Beg with next row 1, BO 5 sts at beg next 2 rows. Beg with next row (WS), dec 1 st each edge every WS row 4 times—73 (85, 97) sts. Cont in patt as set without further shaping until 11 (13, 15) patt sets have been worked. Rep patt rows 1–4 once more.

Armhole Shaping—Detailed

5th (6th, 7th) patt set

Row 1: BO 5 sts, purl to end.

Row 2: BO 5 sts, K1, *6-st rep*, end last rep K2.

Row 3: P2tog tbl, purl to last 2 sts, P2tog.

Row 4: K2tog, *6-st rep*, end last rep ssk.

Row 5: P2tog tbl, purl to last 2 sts, P2tog.

Row 6: K3, K2tog, YO, K1, *6-st rep*, YO, ssk, K3.

Row 7: P2tog tbl, purl to last 2 sts, P2tog.

Row 8: K3, YO, K3, *6-st rep*, YO, sskp.

6th (7th, 8th) patt set

Row 1: P2tog tbl, purl to last 2 sts, P2tog.

Row 2: K2, YO, ssk, K1, *6-st rep*, end last rep K3.

Row 3 (and all rem WS rows): Purl.

Row 4: K3, YO, sskp, *6-st rep*, YO, K1.

Row 6: K2, K2tog, YO, K1, *6-st rep*, YO, ssk.

Row 8: K1, ssk, YO, K3, *6-st rep*, end last rep K4.

Rep last patt set 5 (6, 7) times, purling row 1 without dec, until 11 (13, 15) patt sets have been completed from beg. Work rows 1–4 once more. Back meas approx 10¼ (12, 13¾)"—73 (85, 97) sts.

Follow shoulder shaping for garment size, as indicated below.

Shoulder Shaping (Small)

Row 5: BO 8 sts, purl to end.

Row 6: BO 8 sts, K2, *6-st rep*.

Row 7: BO 8 sts, purl to end.

Row 8: BO 8 sts, K1, *6-st rep*, YO, ssk, K1.

Row 1: BO 7 sts, purl to end.

Row 2: BO 7 sts, K2, YO, ssk, K1, *6-st rep*, K2tog, YO, K1.

Next row, BO rem 27 sts for back neck.

Shoulder Shaping (Medium)

Row 5: BO 10 sts, purl to end.

Row 6: BO 10 sts, *6-st rep*, YO, ssk, K2.

Row 7: BO 10 sts, purl to end.

Row 8: BO 10 sts, K3, *6-st rep*, end last rep K2.

Row 1: BO 9 sts, purl to end.

Row 2: BO 9 sts, K2, YO, ssk, K1, *6-st rep*, K2tog, YO, K1.

Next row, BO rem 27 sts for back neck.

Shoulder Shaping (Large)

Row 5: BO 12 sts, purl to end.

Row 6: BO 12 sts, K1, K2tog, YO, K1, *6-st rep*, YO, ssk.

Row 7: BO 12 sts, purl to end.

Row 8: BO 12 sts, ssk, YO, K3, *6-st rep*, end last rep K4.

Row 1: BO 11 sts, purl to end.

Row 2: BO 11 sts, K2, YO, ssk, K1, *6-st rep*, K2tog, YO, K1.

Next row, BO rem 27 sts for back neck.

RIGHT FRONT

CO 49 (55, 61) sts and work the 8 rows of *mini leaf stitch* 4 (5, 6) times. Front meas approx 3½ (4½, 5¼)" from beg.

Armhole and Neck Shaping—General

BO 5 sts at beg of next row 1. Dec 1 st at armhole edge every WS row 4 times—40 (46, 52) sts. *Note:* Last armhole dec is worked on same row as first neck dec.

Beg with row 1 of next patt set, dec 1 st at neck edge on alt 2nd and 4th WS rows until 17 dec have been worked—23 (29, 35) sts. Cont in patt as set without further shaping until 11 (13, 15) patt sets have been worked. Then work rows 1–4 once more.

Armhole Shaping—Detailed Row by Row

5th (6th, 7th) patt set

Row 1: BO 5 sts, purl to end.

Row 2: K1, *6-st rep*, end last rep K2.

Row 3: P2tog tbl, purl to end.

Row 4: K2tog, *6-st rep*, end last rep ssk.

Row 5: P2tog tbl, purl to end.

Row 6: K1, *6-st rep*, YO, ssk, K3.

Row 7: P2tog tbl, purl to end.

Row 8: K2, *6-st rep*, end YO, ssk, K1—41 (47, 53) sts.

Neck Shaping—Detailed

Work final armhole dec and first neck dec on row 1 as indicated. Rem neck dec are noted at beg of each patt set. Purl WS rows, working dec rows as foll: Purl to last 2 sts, P2tog.

6th (7th, 8th) patt set

Dec on rows 1, 3, and 7.

Row 1: P2tog tbl, purl to last 2 sts, P2tog.

Row 2: *6-st rep*, K2tog, YO, K1.

Row 4: K3, YO, sskp, *6-st rep*, YO, K2.

Row 6: K2, K2tog, YO, K1, *6-st rep*, YO, ssk, K1.

Row 8: Ssk, YO, K3, *6-st rep*, YO, ssk.

7th (8th, 9th) patt set

Dec on rows 1, 5, and 7.

Row 2: K3, *6-st rep*, K2tog, YO, K1.

Row 4: K1, YO, sskp, *6-st rep*, YO, K2.

Row 6: K2, *6-st rep*, YO, ssk, K1.

Row 8: K2, *6-st rep*, YO, ssk.

8th (9th, 10th) patt set

Dec on rows 3 and 5.

Row 2: K1, *6-st rep*, K2tog, YO, K1.

Row 4: K4, YO, sskp, *6-st rep*, YO, K2.

Row 6: K2, K2tog, YO, K1, *6-st rep*, YO, ssk, K1.

Row 8: K1, ssk, YO, K3, *6-st rep*, YO, ssk.

9th (10th, 11th) patt set

Dec on rows 1, 3, and 7.

Row 2: K1, YO, ssk, K1, *6-st rep*, K2tog, YO, K1.

Row 4: K1, YO, sskp, *6-st rep*, YO, K2.

Row 6: K2tog, YO, K1, *6-st rep*, YO, ssk, K1.

Row 8: K3, *6-st rep*, YO, ssk.

10th (11th, 12th) patt set

Dec on rows 1, 5, and 7.

Row 2: K1, *6-st rep*, K2tog, YO, K1.

Row 4: K2tog, *6-st rep*, YO, K2.

Row 6: K3, K2tog, YO, K1, *6-st rep*, YO, ssk, K1.

Row 8: K1, ssk, YO, K3, *6-st rep*, YO, ssk.

11th (12th, 13th) patt set

Dec on rows 3 and 5.

Row 2: K2, YO, ssk, K1, *6-st rep*, K2tog, YO, K1.

Row 4: K2, YO, sskp, *6-st rep*, YO, K2.

Row 6: K2tog, YO, K1, *6-st rep*, YO, ssk, K1.

Row 8: K4, *6-st rep*, YO, ssk.

12th (13th, 14th) patt set

Dec on row 1.

Row 2: K2, *6-st rep*, K2tog, YO, K1.

Row 4: K1, ssk, *6-st rep*, YO, K2.

Size Small only: Beg shoulder shaping now. Front meas approx 10¼"—23 sts.

Row 6: K2, *6-st rep*, YO, ssk, K1.

Row 8: K3, *6-st rep*, YO, ssk.

Size Medium only: Rep Rows 1–4, purling row 1 without dec; then beg shoulder shaping. Front meas approx 12"—29 sts.

Size Large only: Rep last patt set 1 time, purling row 1 without dec. Rep rows 1–4 once more, then beg shoulder shaping. Front meas approx 13¾"—35 sts.

Shoulder Shaping (Small)

Row 5: BO 8 sts, purl to end.

Row 6: K2, *6-st rep*, end last rep K2.

Row 7: BO 8 sts, purl to end.

Row 8: K3, YO, sskp, YO, K1.

Next row, BO rem 7 sts.

Shoulder Shaping (Medium)

Row 5: BO 10 sts, purl to end.

Row 6: K2, *6-st rep*, YO, ssk, K3.

Row 7: BO 10 sts, purl to end.

Row 8: K3, *6-st rep*.

Next row, BO rem 9 sts.

Shoulder Shaping (Large)

Row 5: BO 12 sts, purl to end.

Row 6: K2, *6-st rep*, YO, ssk, K1.

Row 7: BO 12 sts, purl to end.

Row 8: K3, *6-st rep*, YO, ssk.

Next row, BO rem 11 sts.

LEFT FRONT

CO 49 (55, 61) sts and work the 8 rows of *mini leaf stitch* 4 (5, 6) times. Front meas approx 3½ (4½, 5¼)" from beg.

Armhole and Neck Shaping—General

On next row 2, BO 5 sts. Dec 1 st at armhole edge every WS row 4 times—40 (46, 52) sts. *Note:* Last armhole dec is worked on same row as first neck dec.

Beg with row 1 of next patt set, dec 1 st at neck edge on alt 2nd and 4th WS rows until 17 dec have been worked—23 (29, 35) sts. Cont in patt as set without further shaping until 11 (13, 15) patt sets have been worked. Then work rows 1–4 once more.

Armhole Shaping—Detailed

5th (6th, 7th) patt set

Row 1: Purl.

Row 2: BO 5 sts, K1, *6-st rep*.

Row 3: Purl to last 2 sts, P2tog.

Row 4: Ssk, *6-st rep*, end last rep ssk.

Row 5: Purl to last 2 sts, P2tog.

Row 6: K3, K2tog, YO, K1, *6-st rep*.

Row 7: Purl to last 2 sts, P2tog.

Row 8: K1, ssk, YO, K3, *6-st rep*, end last rep K2—41 (47, 53) sts.

Neck Shaping—Detailed

Work final armhole dec and first neck dec on row 1 as indicated. Rem neck dec are noted at beg of each patt set. Purl WS rows, working dec rows as foll: P2tog tbl, purl to end.

6th (7th, 8th) patt set

Dec on rows 1, 3, and 7.

Row 1: P2tog tbl, purl to last 2 sts, P2tog.

Row 2: K1, YO, ssk, K1, *6-st rep*, K2tog, YO, K1, YO, ssk.

Row 4: K2, YO, sskp, *6-st rep*, YO, K3.

Row 6: K1, K2tog, YO, K1, *6-st rep*, YO, ssk, K2.

Row 8: Ssk, YO, K3, *6-st rep*, YO, ssk.

7th (8th, 9th) patt set

Dec on rows 1, 5, and 7.

Row 2: K1, YO, ssk, K1, *6-st rep*, end last rep K3.

Row 4: K2, YO, sskp, *6-st rep*, YO, K1.

Row 6: K1, K2tog, YO, K1, *6-st rep*, end last rep K2.

Row 8: Ssk, YO, K3, *6-st rep*, YO, sskp, YO, K2.

8th (9th, 10th) patt set

Dec on rows 3 and 5.

Row 2: K1, YO, ssk, K1, *6-st rep*.

Row 4: K2, YO, sskp, *6-st rep*, YO, K4.

Row 6: K1, K2tog, YO, K1, *6-st rep*, YO, ssk, K2.

Row 8: Ssk, YO, K3, *6-st rep*, YO, ssk, K1.

9th (10th, 11th) patt set

Dec on rows 1, 3, and 7.

Row 2: K1, YO, ssk, K1, *6-st rep*, K2tog, YO, K1.

Row 4: K2, YO, sskp, *6-st rep*, YO, K1.

Row 6: K1, K2tog, YO, K1, *6-st rep*, YO, ssk.

Row 8: Ssk, YO, K3, *6-st rep*.

SEVILLE

10th (11th, 12th) patt set

Dec on rows 1, 5, and 7.

Row 2: K1, YO, ssk, K1, *6-st rep*.

Row 4: K2, YO, sskp, *6-st rep*, end last rep ssk.

Row 6: K1, K2tog, YO, K1, *6-st rep*, YO, ssk, K3.

Row 8: Ssk, YO, K3, *6-st rep*, YO, ssk, K1.

11th (12th, 13th) patt set

Dec on rows 3 and 5.

Row 2: K1, YO, ssk, K1, *6-st rep*, K2tog, YO, K2.

Row 4: K2, YO, sskp, *6-st rep*, YO, K2.

Row 6: K1, K2tog, YO, K1, *6-st rep*, YO, ssk.

Row 8: Ssk, YO, K3, *6-st rep*, end last rep K4.

12th (13th, 14th) patt set

Dec on row 1 only.

Row 2: K1, YO, ssk, K1, *6-st rep*, end last rep K2.

Row 4: K2, YO, sskp, *6-st rep*, YO, K3, YO, ssk, K1.

Size Small only: Beg shoulder shaping now. Front meas approx 10¼"—23 sts.

Row 6: K1, K2tog, YO, K1, *6-st rep*, end last rep K2.

Row 8: Ssk, YO, K3, *6-st rep*.

Size Medium only: Rep rows 1–4, purling row 1 without dec; then beg shoulder shaping. Front meas approx 12"—29 sts.

Size Large only: Rep last patt set 1 time, purling row 1 without dec. Rep rows 1–4 once more, then beg shoulder shaping. Front meas approx 13¾"—35 sts.

Shoulder Shaping (Small)

Row 5 (and all rem WS rows): Purl.

Row 6: BO 8 sts, K1, *6-st rep*, end last rep K2.

Row 8: BO 8 sts, *6-st rep*.

Next row, BO rem 7 sts.

Shoulder Shaping (Medium)

Row 5 (and all rem WS rows): Purl.

Row 6: BO 10 sts, K2, K2tog, YO, K1, *6-st rep*, end last rep K2.

Row 8: BO 10 sts, K2, *6-st rep*.

Next row, BO rem 9 sts.

Shoulder Shaping (Large)

Row 5 (and all rem WS rows): Purl.

Row 6: BO 12 sts, K2tog, YO, K1, *6-st rep*, end last rep K2.

Row 8: BO 12 sts, K4, *6-st rep*.

Next row, BO rem 11 sts.

SLEEVES

Note: CO provides for 1 selvage st at each edge. Keep selvage sts in *St st*.

CO 39 (39, 45) sts and beg working *mini leaf stitch*.

Sleeve Shaping—General

Work 2 patt sets even. Then, beg with row 1 of 3rd patt set, inc 1 st each edge on alt 8th and 10th rows until 14 inc rows have been worked—67 (67, 73) sts. Cont in patt as set without further shaping until sleeve meas approx 16 (17, 17)", ending with row 8.

Sleeve Shaping—Detailed

Work first 2 patt sets even. Beg with 3rd patt set, purl all WS rows, inc 1 st at each edge on WS rows as noted at beg of each patt set.

1st patt set

No increases.

Row 2: K2, *6-st rep*, end last rep K2.

Row 4: K1, ssk, *6-st rep*, end last rep ssk, K1.

Row 6: K2, *6-st rep*, end last rep K2.

Row 8: K3, *6-st rep*.

2nd patt set

Rep 1st patt set (no increases).

3rd patt set

Inc on row 1.

Row 2: K3, *6-st rep*, end last rep K3.

Row 4: K1, YO, sskp, *6-st rep*, YO, K1.

Row 6: K2tog, YO, K1, *6-st rep*, end last rep K3.

Row 8: K4, *6-st rep*, end last rep K4.

4th patt set

Inc on row 1.

Row 2: K1, YO, ssk, K1, *6-st rep*, K2tog, YO, K1.

Row 4: K2, YO, sskp, *6-st rep*, YO, K2.

Row 6: K1, K2tog, YO, K1, *6-st rep*, YO, ssk, K1.

Row 8: Ssk, YO, K3, *6-st rep*, YO, ssk.

5th patt set

Inc on row 3.

Row 2: K1, YO, ssk, K1, *6-st rep*, K2tog, YO, K1.

Row 4: K3, YO, sskp, *6-st rep*, YO, K3.

Row 6: K2, K2tog, YO, K1, *6-st rep*, YO, ssk, K2.

Row 8: K1, ssk, YO, K3, *6-st rep*, YO, ssk, K1.

6th patt set

Inc on row 3.

Row 2: K2, YO, ssk, K1, *6-st rep*, K2tog, YO, K2.

Row 4: K4, YO, sskp, *6-st rep*, YO, K4.

Row 6: K3, K2tog, YO, K1, *6-st rep*, YO, ssk, K3.

Row 8: K1, *6-st rep*, end last rep K1.

7th patt set

Inc on row 5.

Row 2: *6-st rep*, K2tog, YO, K1, YO, ssk.

Row 4: K4, YO, sskp, *6-st rep*, YO, K4.

Row 6: K1, *6-st rep*.

Row 8: K2, *6-st rep*, end last rep K2.

8th patt set

Inc on row 5.

Row 2: K1, *6-st rep*.

Row 4: Ssk, *6-st rep*, end last rep ssk.

Row 6: K2, *6-st rep*, end last rep K2.

Row 8: K3, *6-st rep*.

9th patt set

Inc on row 7.

Row 2: K2, *6-st rep*, end last rep K2.

Row 4: K1, ssk, *6-st rep*, YO, K3, YO, ssk, K1.

Row 6: K2, *6-st rep*, end last rep K2.

Row 8: K4, *6-st rep*, end last rep K4.

10th patt set

Inc on row 7.

Row 2: K3, *6-st rep*, end last rep K3.

Row 4: K1, YO, sskp, *6-st rep*, YO, K1.

Row 6: K2tog, YO, K1, *6-st rep*, YO, ssk.

Row 8: Ssk, YO, K3, *6-st rep*, YO, ssk.

11th patt set

No increases.

Row 2: K1, YO, ssk, K1, *6-st rep*, K2tog, YO, K1.

Row 4: K2, YO, sskp, *6-st rep*, YO, K2.

Row 6: K1, K2tog, YO, K1, *6-st rep*, YO, ssk, K1.

Row 8: Ssk, YO, K3, *6-st rep*, YO, ssk.

12th patt set

Inc on row 1.

Row 2: K2, YO, ssk, K1, *6-st rep*, K2tog, YO, K2.

Row 4: K3, YO, sskp, *6-st rep*, YO, K3.

Row 6: K2, K2tog, YO, K1, *6-st rep*, YO, ssk, K2.

Row 8: K1, ssk, YO, K3, *6-st rep*, YO, ssk, K1.

13th patt set

Inc on row 1.

Row 2: *6-st rep*, K2tog, YO, K1, YO, ssk.

Row 4: K4, YO, sskp, *6-st rep*, YO, K4.

Row 6: K3, K2tog, YO, K1, *6-st rep*, YO, ssk, K3.

Row 8: K1, *6-st rep*, end last rep K1.

14th patt set

Inc on row 3.

Row 2: *6-st rep*, K2tog, YO, K1, YO, ssk.

Row 4: Ssk, *6-st rep*, end last rep ssk.

Row 6: K1, *6-st rep*.

Row 8: K2, *6-st rep*, end last rep K2.

15th patt set

Inc on row 3.

Row 2: K1, *6-st rep*.

Row 4: K1, ssk, *6-st rep*, YO, K3, YO, ssk, K1.

Row 6: K2, *6-st rep*, end last rep K2.

Row 8: K3, *6-st rep*.

16th patt set

Inc on row 5.

Row 2: K2, *6-st rep*, end last rep K2.

Row 4: K1, ssk, *6-st rep*, YO, K3, YO, ssk, K1.

Row 6: K2tog, YO, K1, *6-st rep*, YO, ssk.

Row 8: K4, *6-st rep*, end last rep K4.

17th patt set

Inc on row 5.

Row 2: K3, *6-st rep*, end last rep K3.

Row 4: K1, YO, sskp, *6-st rep*, YO, K1.

Row 6: K1, K2tog, YO, K1, *6-st rep*, YO, ssk, K1.

Row 8: Ssk, YO, K3, *6-st rep*, YO, ssk.

18th patt set

No increases.

Row 2: K1, YO, ssk, K1, *6-st rep*, K2tog, YO, K1.

Row 4: K2, YO, sskp, *6-st rep*, YO, K2.

Row 6: K1, K2tog, YO, K1, *6-st rep*, YO, ssk, K1.

Row 8: Ssk, YO, K3, *6-st rep*, YO, ssk.

Size Small only: Beg cap shaping now. Sleeve meas approx 16"—67 sts.

Medium and Large only: 19th patt set

No increases.

Row 2: K1, YO, ssk, K1, *6-st rep*, K2tog, YO, K1.

Row 4: K2, YO, sskp, *6-st rep*, YO, K2.

Row 6: K1, K2tog, YO, K1, *6-st rep*, YO, ssk, K1.

Row 8: Ssk, YO, K3, *6-st rep*, YO, ssk.

Sleeve measures approx 17"—67 (73) sts.

Cap Shaping—General

Beg with patt row 1, BO 5 sts beg next 2 rows. Beg with next WS row, dec 1 st each edge every WS row 17 (19, 20) times—23 (19, 23) sts. BO rem sts. Sleeve meas approx 20½ (21¼, 22¼)".

Cap Shaping—Detailed

19th (20th, 20th) patt set

Row 1: BO 5 sts, purl to end.

Row 2: BO 5 sts, K1, YO, ssk, K1, *6-st rep*, K2tog, YO, K2—57 (57, 63) sts.

Row 3: P2tog tbl, purl to last 2 sts, P2tog. Rep this dec row every WS row 16 (18, 19) times—23 (19, 23) sts.

Row 4: K2, YO, sskp, *6-st rep*, YO, K2.

Row 6: K2tog, YO, K1, *6-st rep*, YO, ssk.

Row 8: K3, *6-st rep*.

20th (21st, 21st) patt set

Row 2: K1, *6-st rep*.

Row 4: K4, YO, sskp, *6-st rep*, YO, K4.

Row 6: K2, K2tog, YO, K1, *6-st rep*, YO, ssk, K2.

Row 8: Ssk, YO, K3, *6-st rep*, YO, ssk.

21st (22nd, 22nd) patt set

Row 2: K3, *6-st rep*, end last rep K3.

Row 4: K1, ssk, *6-st rep*, YO, K3, YO, ssk, K1.

Row 6: K1, *6-st rep*.

Row 8: K1, *6-st rep*, end last rep K1.

22nd (23rd, 23rd) patt set

Row 2: K2, YO, ssk, K1, *6-st rep*, K2tog, YO, K2.

Row 4: K2, YO, sskp, *6-st rep*, YO, K2.

Row 6: K2tog, YO, K1, *6-st rep*, YO, ssk.

Row 8: K3, *6-st rep*.

23rd (24th, 24th) patt set

Row 2: K1, *6-st rep*.

Row 4: K4, YO, sskp, *6-st rep*, YO, K4.

Size Small only: BO rem 23 sts next RS row. Sleeve meas approx 20½".

Row 6: K2, K2tog, YO, K1, *6-st rep*, YO, ssk, K2.

Row 8: Ssk, YO, K3, *6-st rep*, YO, ssk.

Size Medium only: BO rem 19 sts next RS row. Sleeve meas approx 21¼".

Size Large only: 25th patt set

Row 2: K3, *6-st rep*, end last rep K3.

Row 4: K1, YO, sskp, *6-st rep*, YO, K1.

Row 6: K2tog, YO, K1, *6-st rep*, end last rep K3.

Row 8: K4, *6-st rep*, end last rep K4.

BO rem 23 sts next RS row. Sleeve meas approx 22¼".

FINISHING

Weave in ends. Block to finished dimensions in schematic. Sew shoulder seams. Sew sleeves in place. Sew underam and side seams.

Picot Edging

With crochet hook and RS facing, beg at bottom right-front edge, work 1 row *sc* along right-front edge, around back neck, and down left front. Ch 1 and turn. Work 2nd row as foll: *sc 5, ch 2, sc in last sc worked; rep from * to bottom right-front edge. Do not break yarn.

Shell-Stitch Hem

Cont with same yarn, work *shell st* directly into CO row from right to left as foll: *sc 3 or 4, skip 1 or 2 sts, dc 5 in next st, skip 1 or 2 sts; rep from * to end. Fasten off.

Note: When working *shell st* hem, add or subtract a sc or skipped st to match the shell scallop (dc 5) to the widest part of the *mini leaf stitch* patt.

Rep *shell st* for sleeve cuffs. Weave in rem ends.

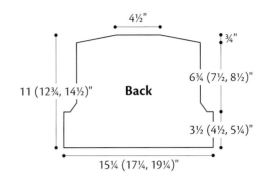

Back

4½"
¾"
11 (12¾, 14½)"
6¾ (7½, 8½)"
3½ (4½, 5¼)"
15¼ (17¼, 19¼)"

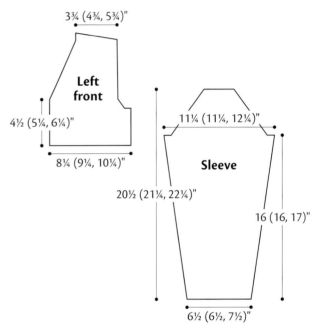

3¾ (4¾, 5¾)"

Left front

4½ (5¼, 6¼)"
8¼ (9¼, 10¼)"

11¼ (11¼, 12¼)"

Sleeve

20½ (21¼, 22¼)"
16 (16, 17)"
6½ (6½, 7½)"

Note: Block to measurements above.

Mini Leaf Stitch

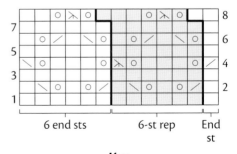

6 end sts   6-st rep   End st

Key

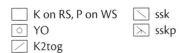

☐ K on RS, P on WS	⟍ ssk
○ YO	⤨ sskp
⟋ K2tog	

Note: Pattern begins on WS row, reading row 1 from left to right.

Captiva

Show off sun-tanned shoulders in this simple summer tank. It's quick to knit, and the raglan shaping and attached I-cord straps are done so neatly, finishing is a breeze. Even beginners will be wearing this in no time.

Skill Level
Beginner

Finished Measurements
Bust: 30½ (32¾, 35, 37¼, 39½, 42)"
Length: 19 (20, 20¾, 21½, 22¼, 23)" approx length with straps
Allow about 0" to 1" of negative ease for a close fit.

Yarn
400 (450, 500, 550, 600, 650) yds worsted-weight yarn.

This look is shown in *Cotton Supreme* from Universal Yarn (100% cotton; 180 yds/165 m; 100 g) in color 502, White: 3 (3, 4, 4, 4, 4) skeins. [4]

Gauge
21 sts and 26 rows = 4" over *St st*

Needles
Size 7 (4.5mm) needles for body and same size dpns for I-cord straps, or size needed to obtain gauge

Notions
Tapestry needle, stitch holders

STITCH GUIDE
K1xP1 Rib (even number of sts)
All rows: *K1, P1; rep from * to end.

PATTERN NOTES
See "Techniques" on page 91 for help with the three-needle bind off (3-needle BO) and I-cord.

BACK
CO 82 (88, 94, 100, 106, 112) sts. Work in *K1xP1 rib* for 4 rows. Next row (RS), beg *St st* (knit on RS rows, purl on WS rows) and work even until back meas 11 (11½, 12, 12½, 13, 13½)" or to desired length, ending with a WS row.

Armhole Shaping
BO 2 (2, 2, 2, 3, 3) sts beg of next 2 rows. Beg with next row (RS), dec as foll: *K1, ssk, knit to last 3 sts, K2tog, K1. Next row, P1, P2tog, purl to last 3 sts, ssp; rep from * 13 (14, 15, 16, 17, 18) times more—22 (24, 26, 28, 28, 30) sts. Place sts on st holder.

FRONT
Work as for back through last dec row—22 (24, 26, 28, 28, 30) sts. Next row (RS), K3, join new yarn, and BO 16 (18, 20, 22, 22, 24) sts for front neck, knit to end—3 sts rem at each edge for straps.

STRAPS

Working straps separately, slip sts for left strap to holder and with RS facing, sl 3 sts for right strap to dpn. *Work I-cord for approx 6" to 8". Do not BO. Do not break yarn. Slip sts to holder.* Slip sts for left strap to dpn, join new yarn, and rep from * to * for left strap.

FINISHING

Weave in ends. Sew side seams. Baste or pin straps to back and try on to determine final strap length. Adjust strap length as desired. With strap length set, slip back sts from holder to needle. Work *3-needle BO* to join one strap with first 3 sts of back. Cont with regular 2-needle BO across center 16 (18, 20, 22, 22, 24) sts of back. Work *3-needle BO* to join rem 3 back sts to sts for second strap. Weave in rem ends securely.

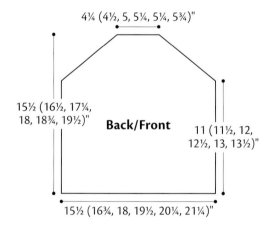

4¼ (4½, 5, 5¼, 5¼, 5¾)"

15½ (16½, 17¼, 18, 18¾, 19½)"

Back/Front

11 (11½, 12, 12½, 13, 13½)"

15½ (16¾, 18, 19½, 20¼, 21¼)"

Fitzroy

For me, the cardigan is a wardrobe essential and
this is one of my favorites. I grab it on the way out
the door to ward off the chill of air conditioning or
wear it on its own, buttoned up over a camisole.

Skill Level

Intermediate

Finished Measurements

Bust: 30¼ (32½, 35¼, 37½, 40½)", buttoned

Length: 18 (18½, 19, 19½, 20)"

Allow about 2" of ease for a standard fit.

Yarn

800 (830, 890, 950, 1030) yds worsted-weight yarn.

This look is shown in *Cotonade* from Knit One, Crochet
Too (100% cotton; 83 yds/76 m; 50 g) in color 547 Stone:
10 (10, 11, 12, 13) balls. ④

Gauge

18 sts and 25 rows = 4" over *vine stripe* patt;
16 sts = 4" over *St st*

Needles

Size 8 (5mm), or size needed to obtain gauge

Notions

Tapestry needle, stitch holders, stitch markers, five
⅝"-diameter buttons

STITCH GUIDE

K2xP2 Rib (multiple of 4 sts + 2)

Row 1 (WS): P2, *K2, P2; rep from * to end.

Row 2: K2, *P2, K2; rep from * to end.

Repeat rows 1 and 2 for pattern.

Vine Stripe

See charts on page 69.

PATTERN NOTES

See "Techniques" on page 91 for help with the three-
needle bind off (3-needle BO).

BACK

CO 74 (78, 86, 90, 98) sts. Beg with a WS row, work 4
rows of *K2xP2 rib*. Next row (WS), purl across row 1
of *Back* chart while dec 2 (0, 3, 1, 2) sts evenly across
row—72 (78, 83, 89, 96) sts. Cont working patt from
chart without further shaping until back meas 18 (18½,
19, 19½, 20)" from beg. (*Note:* It might be helpful to
place markers between each patt rep. Note that the 7-st
patt is worked only on size Small on back.) BO on a
WS row.

RIGHT FRONT

Note: Buttonholes are worked at set intervals. Read ahead
to determine when to work buttonholes.

CO 38 (38, 42, 46, 50) sts. Beg with a WS row, work 4
rows of *K2xP2 rib*. Next row (WS), purl across row 1 of
Right Front chart while dec 2 (0, 0, 2, 3) sts evenly across
row—36 (38, 42, 44, 47) sts. Beg next RS row by working
buttonhole as foll: P2, YO, P2tog, cont in patt as set by
chart to end. Cont working 12 rows of chart rep, working
buttonhole row every 14th row 4 times (5 buttonholes have
been worked). When 12-row rep has been worked 5 times,
beg neck shaping. Front meas approx 10½" from beg.

Neck Shaping

Row 1 and all odd-numbered rows (WS): Purl.

Row 2: P4, K2tog, K1, (YO, K1) twice, ssk, K3, K2tog, K1, P2, cont in patt as set to end.

Row 4: P4, K2tog, YO, K3, YO, K1, ssk, K1, K2tog, K1, P2, cont in patt as set to end.

Row 6: P4, K6, YO, K1, SK2P, K1, P2, cont in patt as set to end.

Row 8: P4, K1, ssk, K2, K2tog, YO, K3, P2, cont in patt as set to end.

Row 10: P4, K1, ssk, K1, K2tog, YO, K3, P2, cont in patt as set to end.

Row 12: P4, K1, K3tog, K1, YO, K3, P2, cont in patt as set to end.

Row 2: P4, K4, K2tog, K1, P2, cont in patt as set to end.

Row 4: P4, K3, K2tog, K1, P2, cont in patt as set to end.

Row 6: P4, K1, ssk, K2, P2, cont in patt as set to end.

Row 8: P4, ssk, K2, P2, cont in patt as set to end.

Row 10: P4, ssk, K1, P2, cont in patt as set to end.

Row 12: P4, ssk, P2, cont in patt as set to end.

Row 2: P4, ssk, P1, cont in patt as set to end.

Row 4: P4, ssk, cont in patt as set to end—22 (24, 28, 30, 33) sts.

Cont in patt as set without further shaping until front meas 18 (18½, 19, 19½, 20)", ending with a RS row. Next row (WS), BO to last 4 sts, do not break yarn, sl rem 4 sts to holder for buttonhole band.

LEFT FRONT

CO 38 (38, 42, 46, 50) sts. Beg with a WS row, work 4 rows of *K2xP2 rib*. Next row (WS), purl across row 1 of *Left Front* chart while dec 2 (0, 0, 2, 3) sts evenly across row—36 (38, 42, 44, 47) sts. Work 12-row patt rep 5 times, then beg neck shaping. Front meas approx 10½" from beg.

Neck Shaping

Row 1 and all odd-numbered rows (WS): Purl.

Row 2: Work in patt as set to last 19 sts, P2, K3, (YO, K1) twice, ssk, K3, K3tog, P4.

Row 4: Work in patt as set to last 18 sts, P2, (K3, YO) twice, K1, ssk, K3tog, P4.

Row 6: Work in patt as set to last 17 sts, P2, K3, YO, K5, SK2P, P4.

Row 8: Work in patt as set to last 16 sts, P2, K1, ssk, K3, K2tog, K1, YO, K1, P4.

Row 10: Work in patt as set to last 15 sts, P2, K1, ssk, K1, K2tog, K1, YO, K2, P4.

Row 12: Work in patt as set to last 14 sts, P2, K1, K3tog, K1, YO, K3, P4.

Row 2: Work in patt as set to last 13 sts, P2, K3, YO, K1, K3tog, P4.

Row 4: Work in patt as set to last 12 sts, P2, K3, YO, K3tog, P4.

Row 6: Work in patt as set to last 11 sts, P2, K3, K2tog, P4.

Row 8: Work in patt as set to last 10 sts, P2, K1, ssk, K1, P4.

Row 10: Work in patt as set to last 9 sts, P2, K1, ssk, P4.

Row 12: Work in patt as set to last 8 sts, P2, ssk, P4.

Row 2: Work in patt as set to last 7 sts, P1, K2tog, P4.

Row 4: Work in patt as set to last 6 sts, K2tog, P4—22 (24, 28, 30, 33) sts.

Cont in patt as set without further shaping until front meas 18 (18½, 19, 19½, 20)", ending with a RS row. Turn and P4 sts for button band. Sl these 4 sts to holder. BO rem sts across row.

SLEEVES

CO 34 (34, 38, 38, 38) sts. Beg with a WS row, work 4 rows of *K2xP2 rib*. Next row (WS), purl across row 1 of *Sleeve* chart while dec 0 (0, 2, 2, 0) sts evenly across row—34 (34, 36, 36, 38) sts. Work in patt from chart, beg sleeve shaping on row 4.

Sleeve Shaping

Note: Read ahead for sleeve shaping notes.

Beg chart row 4, inc 1 st at each edge every 4th row 3 (4, 7, 10, 14) times, then every 6th row 15 (15, 12, 10, 7) times—70 (72, 74, 76, 80) sts. Work new sts in *St st* (knit on RS, purl on WS) until there are a total of 46 sts. On next RS row, work a *7-st rep* (see *Back* chart) at beg and end of row in place of *St st*. *Note:* Beg *7-st rep* on the same chart row currently being worked. Cont in patt as now set, working new inc sts in *St st* until there are 58 sts. On next RS row, work a *13-st rep* (see *Sleeve* chart) at beg and end of row in place of the *7-st rep* and *St sts* added by inc. *Note:* Beg *13-st rep* on the same chart row currently being worked. Cont in patt as now set, working new sts in *St st*—70 (72, 74, 76, 80) sts. Cont in patt as set without further shaping until sleeve meas 19½ ". BO all sts on a WS row.

FINISHING

Weave in ends. Sew shoulder seams from armhole edge to just before sts held for button bands. Meas 7¾ (8, 8¼, 8½, 9)" from each shoulder seam along front and back armhole edges and PM for sleeve placement. Sew sleeves to body between markers. Sew underarm and side seams.

Buttonhole Band

With WS of right front facing, sl 4 sts from holder to needle and cont working in *garter st* (purl every row) until band fits to center back when slightly stretched.

Button Band

With RS of left front facing, sl 4 sts from holder to needle, join new yarn and cont working in *garter st* until band fits to center back when slightly stretched. Work *3-needle BO* to join bands. Sew band to back neck. Sew buttons to button band opp buttonholes. Weave in rem ends.

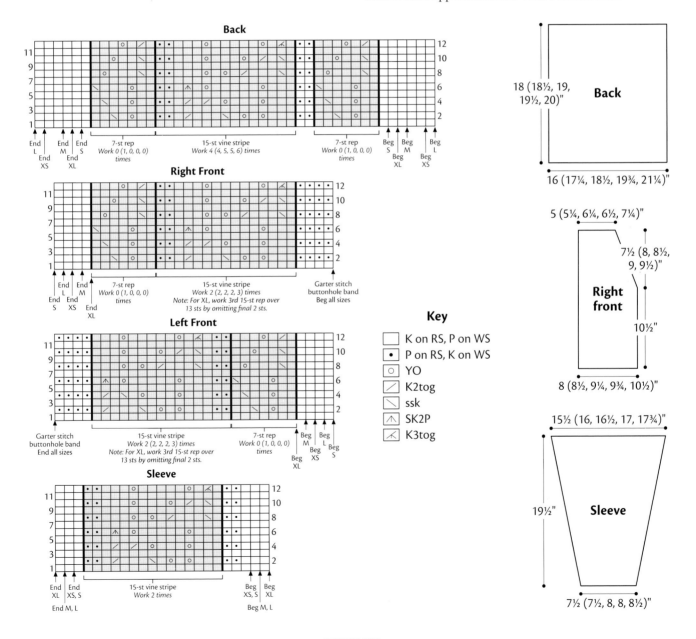

Key

☐	K on RS, P on WS
•	P on RS, K on WS
○	YO
╱	K2tog
╲	ssk
⋀	SK2P
⋏	K3tog

Fall

Bloomsbury

Tiny floral- and leaf-motif stitches add just
a hint of texture to this feminine cardigan.
The swingy A-line and empire waist is flattering
on so many figure types. Just add
a lacy camisole underneath.

Skill Level

Intermediate

Finished Measurements

Bust: 36 (39½, 42¾, 46¼)"

Length: 22 (22¾, 25, 25¾)"

Allow about 2" of ease for a standard fit.

Yarn

1450 (1725, 1975, 2250) yds smooth fingering-weight
yarn.

This look is shown in *Ambrosia* from Knit One, Crochet
Too (70% baby alpaca, 20% silk, 10% cashmere; 137
yds/125 m; 50 g) in color 841 Fawn: 11 (13, 15, 17) balls.

Gauge

28 sts and 36 rows = 4" over *alternating leaf* patt using
larger needles; 28 sts and 32 rows = 4" over *St st*

Needles

Sizes 2 and 3 (2.75 and 3.25mm) needles and size E/4
(3.5 mm) crochet hook, or sizes needed to obtain gauge

Notions

Tapestry needle, three ⅜"-diameter shank-style buttons,
2 (2¼, 2½) yds ¼"-wide satin ribbon

STITCH GUIDE

Charts for both lace patterns are available on page 76.

Alternating Leaf (multiple of 9 sts + 3)

Row 1 (WS): Purl.

Row 2: Knit.

Row 3: Purl.

Row 4: K3, *K2tog, K1, YO, K6, rep from * to end.

Row 5: P1, *P6, YO, P1, P2tog*, rep from * to *, end P2.

Row 6: K1, *K2tog, K1, YO, K6*, rep from * to *, end K2.

Row 7: P3, *P6, YO, P1, P2tog, rep from * to end.

Row 8: Knit.

Row 9: Purl.

Row 10: Knit.

Row 11: Purl.

Row 12: *K6, YO, K1, ssk, rep from * to *, K3.

Row 13: P2, *P2tog tbl, P1, YO, P6*, rep from * to *, P1.

Row 14: K2, *K6, YO, K1, ssk*, rep from * to *, K1.

Row 15: *P2tog tbl, P1, YO, P6*, rep from * to *, P3.

Row 16: Knit.

Repeat rows 1–16 for pattern.

Wildflower Knot

(multiple of 8 sts + 5)

Rows 1, 3, and 5 (WS): Purl.

Rows 2 and 4: Knit.

Row 6: K5, *P3tog, leaving sts on left-hand needle, YO, then purl same 3 sts tog again, K5*.

Rows 7–11: Rep rows 1–5.

Row 12: K1, *P3tog, leaving sts on left-hand needle, YO, then purl same 3 sts tog again, K5; rep from *, end last rep K1.

Repeat rows 1–12 for pattern.

PATTERN NOTES

All lengths referred to in pattern instructions are measured from the *slip-stitch turning row* unless otherwise specified.

The number of cast-on stitches includes one selvage stitch at each edge. Work selvage stitches in *stockinette stitch* unless otherwise instructed.

When shaping on pattern stitches, work a yarn over or decrease only if it can be worked with its companion decrease or yarn over.

See "Techniques" on page 91 for help with crochet basics.

BACK

With smaller needles, CO 140 (149, 158, 167) sts. Beg with a RS row, work in *St st* (knit on RS rows, purl on WS rows) for 1", ending with a WS row. On next row (RS), work *slip stitch turning row* for turned hem as foll: K1 (2, 1, 2), *wyif sl 1, K1; rep from * to last st, K1. Change to larger needles and work *alternating leaf* patt, keeping 1 selvage st at each edge in *St st*. Work even in patt as set until back meas 3½ (4, 4½, 5)" from *slip stitch turning row*, ending with a WS row.

Side Shaping

Next row (RS), dec 1 st at each edge as foll: *K1, ssk, work in patt to last 3 sts, K2tog, K1. Work even in patt as set for 1½", ending with a WS row. Rep from * 3 times more. Rep only dec row once more—130 (139, 148, 157) sts. Cont even in patt as set until back meas approx 11 (12, 13, 13½)", ending with closest patt row 1 or row 9.

Eyelet Row

Next row (RS), work eyelet row as foll: K1 (2, 2, 2), *K2, YO, K2tog; rep from * to last 1 (1, 2, 3) st, knit rem sts. Next row (WS), beg *wildflower knot* patt, dec 3 (4, 5, 6) sts evenly across first row—127 (135, 143, 151) sts including selvage sts. Work even in patt until back meas 12½ (13¼, 14¾, 15½)", ending with a WS row.

Armhole Shaping

BO 7 sts beg next 2 rows. Next row (RS), dec 1 st at each edge as foll: K1, ssk, work in patt to last 3 sts, K2tog, K1. Rep this dec row every RS row 6 (5, 5, 7) times more—99 (109, 117, 121) sts. Cont in patt as set until back meas 20¾ (21½, 23¾, 24½)", ending with a WS row. PM to indicate center 37 (43, 47, 49) sts for back neck.

Neck Shaping

Next row (RS), work to first marker, join new yarn and BO off center 37 (43, 47, 49) sts for back neck, cont in patt to end—31 (33, 35, 36) sts rem for each shoulder. Work both sides of neck at the same time with separate balls of yarn. Next 2 rows, work in patt across first neck edge, BO 2 sts beg of opp neck edge, work in patt to end. Next row (WS), work to 3 sts before first neck edge, P1, ssp, beg opp neck edge P1, P2tog, then cont in patt to end—28 (30, 32, 33) sts rem for each shoulder.

Shoulder Shaping

Beg next 2 rows, BO 10 (10, 11, 11) sts for first shoulder, work to end of opp shoulder. Beg next 2 rows, BO 9 (10, 10, 11) sts at each armhole edge. Then BO rem 9 (10, 10, 11) sts at each armhole edge over next 2 rows.

RIGHT FRONT

With smaller needles, CO 68 (77, 86, 95) sts. Work as for back, keeping 1 selvage st at each edge in *St st*, until piece meas 3½ (4, 4½, 5)", ending with a WS row.

Side Shaping

Next row (RS), *dec 1 st at seam edge as foll: work in patt to last 3 sts, K2tog, K1. Work even in patt as set for 1½", ending with a WS row; rep from * 3 times more. Rep only dec row once more—63 (72, 81, 90) sts. Cont even in patt as set until front meas approx 11 (12, 13, 13½)", ending with closest patt row 1 or row 9 as for back.

Eyelet Row

Next row (RS), work eyelet row as foll: K1 (2, 0, 0), *K2, YO, K2tog; rep from *, K2 (2, 1, 2). Next row (WS), beg *wildflower knot* patt, dec 0 (1, 2, 3) sts evenly across first row—63 (71, 79, 87) sts including selvage sts. Work even in patt until front meas 12½ (13¼, 14¾, 15½)", ending with a RS row.

Armhole and Neck Shaping

Note: Neck shaping beg before armhole shaping is complete.

Next row (WS), BO 7 sts, work in patt to end. Beg next RS row, dec 1 st at armhole edge as foll: work in patt to last 3 sts, K2tog, K1. Rep dec row every RS row 6 (5, 5, 7) times more. AT THE SAME TIME, when front meas 14 (14½, 16, 15¾)", dec 1 st at neck beg next RS row as foll: K1, ssk, work in patt to end. Cont shaping neck every RS row 11 (23, 33, 38) times more, then every 4th row 9 (4, 0, 0) times—28 (30, 32, 33) sts. Cont in patt as set until front meas 21¼ (22¾, 24¼, 25¼)", ending with a RS row.

Shoulder Shaping

Next row (WS), BO 10 (10, 11, 11) sts, work in patt to end. Next WS row, BO 9 (10, 11, 11) sts. Next WS row, BO rem 9 (10, 10, 11) sts.

LEFT FRONT

With smaller needles, CO 68 (77, 86, 95) sts. Work as for back, keeping 1 selvage st at each edge in *St st*, until piece meas 3½ (4, 4½, 5)", ending with a WS row.

Side Shaping

Next row (RS), *dec 1 st at seam edge as foll: K1, ssk, work in patt to end. Work even in patt as set for 1½", ending with a WS row; rep from * 3 times more. Rep only dec row once more—63 (72, 81, 90) sts. Cont even in patt as set until front meas approx 11 (12, 13, 13½)", ending with closest patt row 1 or row 9 as for back.

Eyelet Row

Next row (RS), work eyelet row as foll: K1 (2, 0, 0), *K2, YO, K2tog; rep from *, K2 (2, 1, 2). Next row (WS), beg *wildflower knot* patt, dec 0 (1, 2, 3) sts evenly across first row—63 (71, 79, 87) sts including selvage sts. Work even in patt until front meas 12½ (13¼, 14¾, 15½)", ending with a WS row.

Armhole and Neck Shaping

Note: Neck shaping begs before armhole shaping is complete.

Next row (RS), BO 7 sts, work in patt to end. Next RS row, dec 1 st at armhole edge as foll: K1, ssk, work in patt to end. Rep dec row every RS row 6 (5, 5, 7) times more. AT THE SAME TIME, when front meas 14 (14½, 16, 15¾)", dec 1 st at neck beg next RS row as foll: work in patt to last 3 sts, K2tog, K1. Cont shaping neck every RS row 11 (23, 33, 38) times more, then every 4th row 9 (4, 0, 0) times—28 (30, 32, 33) sts. Cont in patt as set until front meas 21¼ (22¾, 24¼, 25¼)", ending with a WS row.

Shoulder Shaping

Next row (RS), BO 10 (10, 11, 11) sts, work in patt to end. Next (RS) row, BO 9 (10, 11, 11) sts. Next (RS) row, BO rem 9 (10, 10, 11) sts.

SLEEVES

With smaller needles, CO 113 (113, 122, 122) sts. Beg with a RS row, work in *St st* for 1", ending with a WS row. On next row (RS), work *slip stitch turning row* for turned hem as foll: K2 (2, 1, 1), *wyif sl 1, K1; rep from * to last st, K1. Change to larger needles and work *alternating leaf* patt, keeping 1 selvage st at each edge in *St st*. When sleeve meas 2", beg next RS row, inc 1 st at each edge as foll: K1, ssk, work in patt to last 3 sts, K2tog, K1. Rep sleeve inc every 18th row 4 times more—123 (123, 132, 132) sts. Cont even until sleeve meas 11 (11, 11½, 11¾)", ending with a WS row.

Cap Shaping

BO 7 sts beg next 2 rows. Next row (RS), dec 1 st at each edge as foll: K1, ssk, work to last 3 sts, K2tog, K1. Rep this dec row every RS row 9 times more. Then dec 1 st at each edge every row 26 (26, 30, 30) times, working WS row dec as foll: P1, P2tog, work in patt to last 3 sts, ssp, P1—37 (37, 38, 38) sts. BO 5 sts beg next 4 rows. BO rem 17 (17, 18, 18) sts.

FINISHING

Weave in ends. Block all pieces. Sew shoulder seams. Sew sleeves in place. Sew underarm and side seams. Turn up hem of body along *slip stitch turning row* and stitch in place. Rep for sleeve hems.

Picot Edging

With crochet hook and RS facing, beg at right-front hem edge and work 1 row *sc* along right front, around neck and down left front to hem edge, ch 1 and turn. Work back as foll: sl st 3, *(sl st 1, ch 3, sl st 1) in next sc, sl st 3, (sl st 1, ch 3, sl st 1) in next sc, sl st 1, (sl st 1, ch 3, sl st 1) in next sc, sl st 3; rep from * to point on right front where neck shaping beg.

Button Loops

Make 3 button loops evenly spaced on right front between point where neck shaping beg and approx ½" above eyelet row by working ch 5 in place of ch 3 for 3 of the picot points. Cont with picot edging as previously set to right-front hem edge. Fasten off. Sew buttons to left front opp button loops. Weave in rem ends. Thread tapestry needle with ribbon and weave through eyelets.

Alternating Leaf

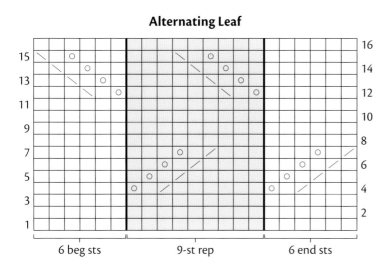

6 beg sts   9-st rep   6 end sts

Note: Both patts beg on WS;
begin row 1 reading from left to right.

Wildflower Knot

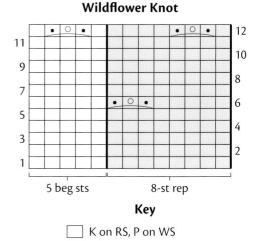

5 beg sts   8-st rep

Key

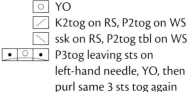

☐ K on RS, P on WS

⊙ YO

╱ K2tog on RS, P2tog on WS

╲ ssk on RS, P2tog tbl on WS

P3tog leaving sts on left-hand needle, YO, then purl same 3 sts tog again

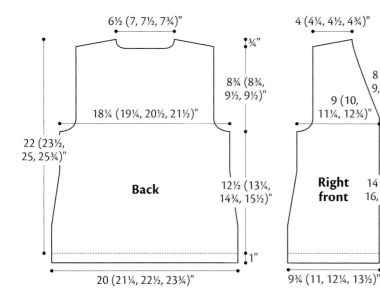

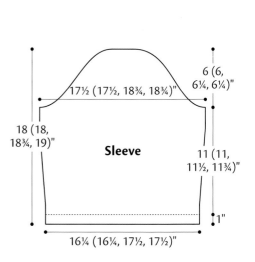

Sienna

This cardigan is a wardrobe workhorse. Knit it in wool or cotton, in a solid color or fabulous hand-painted yarn—you decide what you want it to be. Consider choosing two sets of buttons, one casual and one a bit dressier, and using button pins to easily change them with your mood.

Skill Level

Easy/Intermediate

Finished Measurements

Bust: 35½ (37½, 39¼, 41, 43, 44¾, 46¾)"

Length: 19 (19½, 20, 21½, 21, 21½, 22)"

Allow about 2" of ease for a standard fit.

Yarn

1250 (1350, 1450, 1525, 1640, 1700, 1800) yds worsted-weight yarn.

This look is shown in *King George* from Plymouth Yarns (45% baby alpaca, 45% merino wool, 10% cashmere; 105 yds; 50 g) in color 2878: 12 (13, 14, 15, 16, 17, 18) balls.

Gauge

21½ sts and 28 rows = 4" over *K9xP1 rib*; 20 sts and 28 rows = 4" over *St st*

Needles

Size 7 (4.5mm) 24" circular needles, or size needed to obtain gauge

Notions

Six ⅝"-diameter buttons, stitch markers, tapestry needle

STITCH GUIDE

Gazebo Lace Points** (multiple of 10 sts + 1)

Row 1 (WS): *P5, [make bobble as foll: (K1, P1, K1) in next st, turn work, P1, K1, P1, turn work, K1, P1, K1, then pass 2nd and 3rd sts over 1st st and off right-hand needle], P4; rep from *, end last rep P5.

Row 2: K1, *YO, K3, SK2P, K3, YO, K1; rep from * to end.

Row 3: Purl.

Row 4: K1, *K1, YO, K2, SK2P, K2, YO, K2; rep from * to end.

Row 5: Purl.

Row 6: K1, *K2, YO, K1, SK2P, K1, YO, K3*; rep from * to end.

Row 7: Purl.

Row 8: K1, *K3, YO, SK2P, YO, K4; rep from * to end.

**From Knitting on the Edge *by Nicky Epstein; see* "Bibliography," *page 95.*

K9xP1 Rib (multiple of 10 sts + 1)

Row 1 (WS): P5, K1, *P9, K1; rep from * to last 5 sts, P5.

Row 2: K5, P1, *K9, P1; rep from * to last 5 sts, K5.

Repeat rows 1 and 2 for pattern.

PATTERN NOTES

See "Techniques" on page 91 for help with picking up stitches.

BODY

CO 191 (201, 211, 221, 231, 241, 251) sts and working back and forth in rows, work 8 rows of *gazebo lace points*. Next row (WS), beg *K9xP1 rib* and work in patt until piece meas 11 (11, 11, 11¾, 12, 12, 12¼)" from beg, including points (or to desired length), ending with a WS row. PM for armholes as foll: count 41 (43, 44, 46, 49, 50, 52) sts, PM, count 12 (14, 16, 18, 18, 20, 22) sts, PM, count 85 (87, 91, 93, 97, 101, 103) sts, PM, count 12 (14, 16, 18, 18, 20, 22) sts, PM, 41 (43, 44, 46, 49, 50, 52) sts rem.

Neck and Armhole Shaping

Note: Armhole shaping begins before neck shaping is complete.

Beg next row (RS), shape neck by dec 1 st at each edge every RS row 11 (12, 12, 13, 15, 15, 17) times, then every 4th row 5 times as foll: K1, ssk, work to last 3 sts, K2tog, K1. When piece meas 11½ (11¾, 11¾, 12¼, 12½, 12½, 12¾)" from beg, BO for armholes on next RS row as foll: work in patt as set to first marker, sl sts just worked to holder for right front. BO 12 (14, 16, 18, 18, 20, 22) sts between markers for armhole. Work to third marker, sl sts just worked to holder for back. BO 12 (14, 16, 18, 18, 20, 22) sts between markers for armhole, work to end. Turn and cont in patt as set for left front, working K2tog, K1 at end of each neck shaping row as previously indicated—25 (26, 27, 28, 29, 30, 30) sts rem with neck shaping complete. Cont even until front meas 19 (19½, 20, 20½, 21, 21½, 22)" from beg. BO rem sts in patt.

BACK

Sl 85 (87, 91, 93, 97, 101, 103) sts held for back to needles ready to work a WS row. Join new yarn and cont in patt as set until back meas 19 (19½, 20, 20½, 21, 21½, 22)" from beg. BO rem sts in patt.

RIGHT FRONT

Sl 41 (43, 44, 46, 49, 50, 52) sts held for right front to needles, ready to work a WS row. Cont in patt as set, working K1, ssk at beg of neck shaping rows (RS) as previously indicated—25 (26, 27, 28, 29, 30, 30) sts rem with neck shaping complete. Cont even until front meas 19 (19½, 20, 20½, 21, 21½, 22)" from beg. BO rem sts in patt.

SLEEVES

CO 51 (51, 51, 51, 61, 61, 61) sts and work 8 rows of *gazebo lace points*. Next row (WS), beg *K9xP1 rib* and work in patt until sleeve meas 3½" from beg, including points, ending with a WS row. Beg with next row (RS), inc 1 st at each edge every 6th row 0 (4, 11, 15, 2, 6, 13) times, then every 8th row 15 (12, 7, 4, 14, 11, 6) times, taking new sts into patt as they are added—81 (83, 87, 89, 93, 95, 99) sts. Cont in patt as set without further shaping until sleeve meas 20½" from beg, ending with a WS row. BO all sts in patt.

FINISHING

Weave in ends. Block lightly if desired. Sew shoulder seams. Sew sleeves in place. Sew underarm seams.

Front Bands

PM for buttonholes along right-front edge as foll: PM ½" below point where neck shaping beg, place second marker 1" above the widest part of the diamond formed by *gazebo lace points* and rem markers evenly spaced between these 2 markers. With RS facing and beg at right-front hem edge, pick up approx 3 sts for every 4 rows along right front, 1 st for every BO st across back neck, and 3 sts for every 4 rows along left front. *Knit to marker, YO, K2tog; rep from * for rem markers, knit to end. Next row, BO all sts kwise. Sew buttons opp buttonholes. Weave in rem ends.

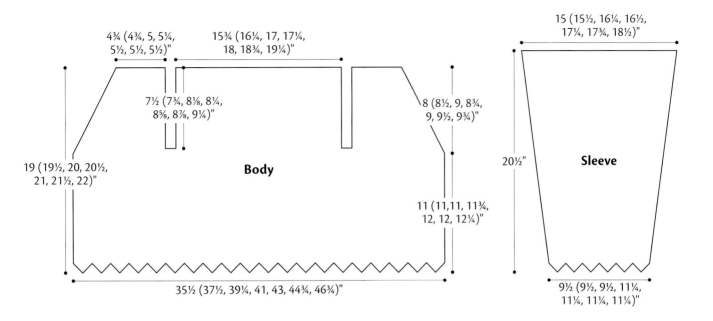

4¾ (4¾, 5, 5¼, 5½, 5½, 5½)"

15¾ (16¼, 17, 17¼, 18, 18¾, 19¼)"

7½ (7¾, 8⅛, 8¼, 8⅝, 8⅞, 9¼)"

8 (8½, 9, 8¾, 9, 9½, 9¾)"

19 (19½, 20, 20½, 21, 21½, 22)"

Body

11 (11, 11, 11¾, 12, 12, 12¼)"

35½ (37½, 39¼, 41, 43, 44¾, 46¾)"

15 (15½, 16¼, 16½, 17¼, 17¾, 18½)"

20½"

Sleeve

9½ (9½, 9½, 11¼, 11¼, 11¼, 11¼)"

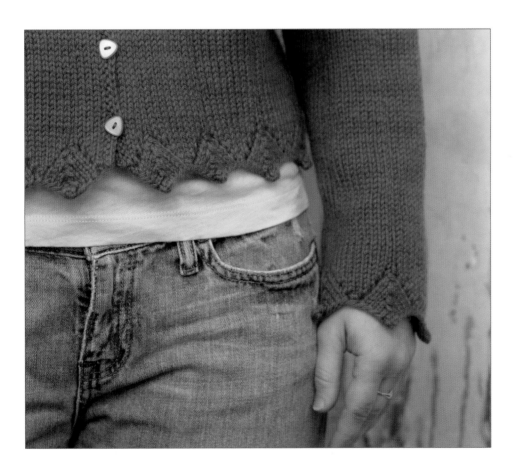

Greenwich

This simple and stylish knitted coat will keep you warm when the weather starts to cool and you just aren't ready to break out your winter coat. The moss-stitch bands at the front edges are worked with the front sections to minimize finishing.

Skill Level

Beginner/Easy

Finished Measurements

Bust: 37¼ (39½, 41¾, 44, 45¾, 48, 50¼)", buttoned

Length: 28 (29, 30, 31, 32, 33, 33½)"

Allow 4" to 5" of ease for an oversized fit.

Yarn

1065 (1155, 1225, 1315, 1415, 1585, 1680) yds smooth, bulky yarn.

This look is shown in *Temptation* from Knit One Crochet Too (50% baby alpaca, 50% merino wool; 55 yds/50 g) in color 800 Camel: 20 (21, 23, 24, 26, 29, 31) balls. (5)

Gauge

14 sts and 19 rows = 4" over *St st*

Needles

Size 10½ (6.5mm) needles and size J/10 (6mm) crochet hook for neck edge, or size needed to obtain gauge

Notions

Tapestry needle, clip-on stitch markers, one 2"-diameter button

STITCH GUIDE

Moss Stitch (even number of sts)

Rows 1 and 2: *K1, P1; rep from * to end.

Rows 3 and 4: *P1, K1; rep from * to end.

Repeat rows 1–4 for pattern.

PATTERN NOTES

The row gauge for both *moss st* and *St st* should match so front bands lie flat.

A coat knit in a bulky yarn can be heavy, so take care when choosing yarn. Avoid 100% cotton at this gauge and instead look for something lofty with more bulk in volume than in weight, such as this luscious merino/alpaca blend.

It's helpful to measure the length of heavy pieces while they're hanging freely, rather than lying flat.

Length can be easily adjusted at any point on the body or sleeves after the *moss stitch* hem edge is worked and before the front neck shaping.

See "Techniques" on page 91 for help with long-tail cast on, backward-loop cast on, and reverse single crochet.

BACK

Using the long-tail method, CO 66 (70, 74, 78, 82, 86, 90) sts. Beg with row 1 as a RS row, work in *moss st*, keeping 1 selvage st at each edge in *St st* (knit on RS, purl on WS), until back meas 4 (4, 4, 4, 5, 5, 5)" from beg, ending with a RS row. Beg with next row (WS), work even in *St st* (knit on RS, purl on WS) until back meas 28 (29, 30, 31, 32, 33, 33½)" from beg. Next row, BO all sts.

RIGHT FRONT

Using the long-tail method, CO 39 (41, 43, 45, 47, 49, 51) sts. Beg with row 1 as a RS row, work in *moss st*, keeping 1 selvage st at seam edge in *St st* (last st of RS rows and first st of WS rows), until front meas 4 (4, 4, 4, 5, 5, 5)", ending with a RS row. Next row (WS), work in *St st*, purling to last 10 (10, 10, 10, 12, 12, 12) sts, PM for front band, then cont in *moss st* as set on previous rows. With patt now set, work 10 (10, 10, 10, 12, 12, 12) sts of *moss st* at beg of RS rows and end of WS rows and *St st* for remainder of each row. Cont even until front meas 24½ (25, 26, 26½, 27½, 28½, 29)" from beg, ending with a WS row.

Buttonhole

Next row (RS), work buttonhole as foll: Work in patt for 4 (4, 4, 4, 5, 5, 5) sts, BO next 3 sts in patt. *Note:* 5 (5, 5, 5, 6, 6, 6) sts on right-hand needle after buttonhole BO. Cont in patt as set to end. Next row (WS), work in patt to bound-off sts, CO 3 sts using the backward-loop method, work in patt to end. Cont even until front meas 26 (26½, 27½, 28, 29, 30, 30½)" from beg, ending with a WS row.

Neck Shaping

Beg next row (RS), BO 10 (10, 10, 10, 12, 12, 12) sts in patt—29 (31, 33, 35, 35, 37, 39) sts. Beg next RS row, BO 3 (3, 3, 3, 3, 3, 4) sts. Beg next RS row, BO 2 (2, 2, 3, 2, 3, 3) sts. Next RS row, K2tog, knit to end—23 (25, 27, 28, 29, 30, 31) sts rem. Cont in patt as set without further shaping until piece meas 28 (29, 30, 31, 32, 33, 33½)" from beg. Next row, BO all sts.

LEFT FRONT

Using the long-tail method, CO 39 (41, 43, 45, 47, 49, 51) sts. Beg with row 1 as a RS row, work in *moss st*, keeping 1 selvage st at side-seam edge in *St st* (first st of RS rows and last st of WS rows), until front meas 4 (4, 4, 4, 5, 5, 5)", ending with a RS row. Next row (WS), work first 10 (10, 10, 10, 12, 12, 12) sts in *moss st* as set on previous rows, PM, cont in *St st* to end. Work in patt as now set, working 10 (10, 10, 10, 12, 12, 12) sts of *moss st* at end of RS and beg of WS rows and *St st* for remainder of each row. Cont even until front meas 26 (26½, 27½, 28, 29, 30, 30½)" from beg, ending with a RS row.

Neck Shaping

Beg next row (WS), BO 10 (10, 10, 10, 12, 12, 12) sts in patt—29 (31, 33, 35, 35, 37, 39) sts. Beg next WS row, BO 3 (3, 3, 3, 3, 3, 4) sts. Beg next WS row, BO 2 (2, 2, 3, 2, 3, 3) sts. Next WS row, P2tog, purl to end—23 (25, 27, 28, 29, 30, 31) sts rem. Cont in patt as set without further shaping until piece meas 28 (29, 30, 31, 32, 33, 33½)" from beg. Next row, BO all sts.

SLEEVES

Using the long-tail method, CO 58 (60, 60, 62, 62, 64, 66) sts. Beg with row 1 as a WS row, work in *moss st*, keeping 1 selvage st at each edge in *St st*, until sleeve meas 4 (4, 4, 4, 5, 5, 5)", ending with a RS row. Beg with next row (WS), work even in *St st* until sleeve meas 16¾ (17, 17, 17, 17½, 17½, 17½)" from beg. Next row, BO all sts.

FINISHING

Weave in ends. Block all pieces. Sew shoulder seams. Meas 8¼ (8½, 8½, 8¾, 8¾, 9, 9½)" from each shoulder seam along front and back armhole edges and PM for sleeve placement. Sew sleeves to body between markers. Sew underarm sleeve seams, reversing seam along *moss st* cuff so seam is hidden within turned-up cuff. Sew side seams. With crochet hook and RS facing, beg at left-front neck edge and work 1 row of *rev sc* around neck edge. Sew button to left front opp buttonhole. Weave in rem ends. Turn up cuffs.

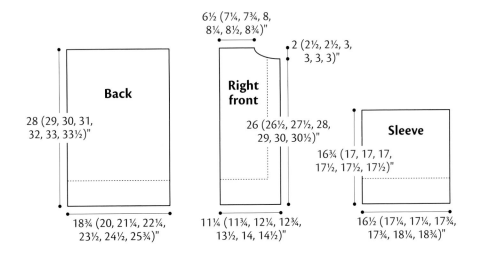

Back

28 (29, 30, 31, 32, 33, 33½)"

18¾ (20, 21¼, 22¼, 23½, 24½, 25¾)"

6½ (7¼, 7¾, 8, 8¼, 8½, 8¾)"

Right front

2 (2½, 2½, 3, 3, 3, 3)"

26 (26½, 27½, 28, 29, 30, 30½)"

11¼ (11¾, 12¼, 12¾, 13½, 14, 14½)"

Sleeve

16¾ (17, 17, 17, 17½, 17½, 17½)"

16½ (17¼, 17¼, 17¾, 17¾, 18¼, 18¾)"

Sedona

The fluted rib stitch used in this sweater creates a wonderfully dimensional fabric. The fun twisted hem and neck treatment add to the look. I've chosen a luxurious fiber with a faint halo that ever so slightly blurs the lines of the stitch pattern. Any crisp wool that shows off your stitches will work beautifully, as will many cottons or blends.

Skill Level

Easy/Intermediate

Finished Measurements

Bust: 36½ (39½, 42¾, 45¾)"

Length: 19 (20, 21, 22)"

Allow 2" to 3" of ease for a standard to loose fit.

Yarn

1200 (1275, 1365, 1465) yds smooth worsted-weight yarn.

This look is shown in *Suri Merino* from Blue Sky Alpacas (60% baby suri, 40% merino; 164 yds/150 m; 100 g) in color 413 Fog: 8 (8, 9, 9) skeins. ⓸

Gauge

21 sts and 28 rows = 4" with larger needles over *fluted rib* smoothed flat slightly by hand

Needles

Size 7 (4.5mm) needles for body and size 6 (4mm) 16" circular needle for neckline, or sizes needed to obtain gauge

Notions

Stitch markers, tapestry needle

STITCH GUIDE

*T-Twist Hem*** (multiple of 6 sts)

Rows 1, 3, and 5 (RS): Knit.

Rows 2, 4, and 6: Purl.

Row 7: K6, *rotate left-hand needle one full turn counterclockwise, K6; rep from * to end.

***From* Knitting on the Edge *by Nicky Epstein; see "Bibliography," page 95.*

Fluted Rib (multiple of 8 sts)

Chart is available on page 89.

Row 1 (RS): *P1, K7; rep from * to end.

Row 2: *K7, P1; rep from * to end.

Row 3: *P1, K7; rep from * to end.

Row 4: K1, *P5, K3; rep from * to last 7 sts, P5, K2.

Row 5: P3, *K3, P5; rep from *, end last rep P2.

Row 6: K3, *P1, K7; rep from *, end last rep K4.

Row 7: K4, *P1, K7; rep from *, end last rep K3.

Row 8: K3, *P1, K7; rep from *, end last rep K4.

Row 9: P3, *K3, P5; rep from *, end last rep P2.

Row 10: K1, *P5, K3; rep from *, end last rep K2.

Repeat rows 1–10 for pattern.

PATTERN NOTES

The accordion effect of the *fluted rib* stitch will cause the finished sweater to appear smaller than it really is. It will open up like an accordion when worn.

The number of stitches includes one selvage stitch at each edge. Work selvage stitches in *stockinette stitch* unless instructed otherwise.

See "Techniques" on page 91 for help with picking up stitches and whipstitching.

BACK

With larger needles, CO 96 (102, 114, 120) sts. Work *T-twist hem*. Next row (WS), purl, inc 2 (4, 0, 2) sts evenly across row—98 (106, 114, 122) sts. Beg with row 3, work in *fluted rib,* keeping selvage sts in *St st*. Cont even until back meas 11¾ (12¾, 13½, 14)" from beginning or to desired length, ending with a WS row.

Armhole Shaping

BO 8 sts beg of next 2 rows—82 (90, 98, 106) sts. Cont even in patt as set, keeping 1 selvage st at each edge, until back meas 18 (19, 20, 21)" from beg, ending with a WS row. Place markers to indicate center 30 (32, 34, 36) sts for back neck.

Neck Shaping

On next row (RS), work to first marker, join new yarn, and BO off center 30 (32, 34, 36) sts; cont in patt to end—26 (29, 32, 35) sts rem for each shoulder. Work both sides of neck at the same time with separate balls of yarn. Next 2 rows, work in patt across first neck edge, BO 2 sts beg opp neck edge, cont in patt to end. Work 1 row even. *On next row (RS), work to 3 sts before first neck edge, K2tog, K1, then beg opp neck edge K1, ssk, work in patt to end. Rep from * 1 time—22 (25, 28, 31) sts each side. Cont even in patt as set until back meas 19 (20, 21, 22)" from beg, ending with a WS row. Next row, BO all sts in patt.

FRONT

Work as for back until front meas 14¼ (15, 15¾, 16½)" from beg, ending with a WS row. PM to indicate center 18 (20, 22, 24) sts for front neck.

Neck Shaping

On next row (RS), work to first marker, join new yarn, and BO off center 18 (20, 22, 24) sts for front neck, cont in patt to end—26 (29, 32, 35) sts rem for each shoulder. Work both sides of neck at the same time with separate balls of yarn. Next 2 rows, work in patt across first neck edge, BO 2 sts beg opp neck edge, cont in patt to end. Work 1 row even. On next row (RS), *work to 3 sts before first neck edge, K2tog, K1, then beg opp neck edge, K1, ssk, work in patt to end. Rep from * every RS row 4 times more, then every 4th row 2 times, and then every 6th row once more—22 (25, 28, 31) sts rem each side. Cont even in patt as set until front meas same as back, ending with same WS patt row as back. Next row, BO all sts in patt.

SLEEVES

With larger needles, CO 66 sts for all sizes. Work *T-twist hem*. Next row (WS), purl. Keeping 1 selvage st at each edge in *St st*, beg with row 3 and work in *fluted rib* for 6 (6, 5, 3)", ending with a WS row.

Sleeve Shaping

Next RS row, K1f&b into selvage st, PM to indicate beg of stitch repeat, and cont in patt to last st, PM, K1f&b. With markers now in place, work inc row every 12th row 0 (0, 4, 9) times as foll: K1, K1f&b, work in patt to last 2 sts, K1f&b, K1. Then rep inc row every 16th row 5 (5, 3, 0) times—78 (78, 82, 86) sts. *Note:* Take new sts into patt while keeping 1 selvage st at each edge in *St st*. Cont even until sleeve meas 18¾", or to desired length, ending with a WS row. BO all sts in patt.

FINISHING

Weave in ends. To retain dimensional effect, do not block, or block very lightly. Sew shoulder seams. Sew sleeves in place. Sew underarm and side seams. With circular needle and RS facing, beg at right shoulder seam and pick up approx 3 sts for every 4 rows along shaped neck edges and 1 st for every BO st around neck, PM, and join. Knit 6 rnds. Next rnd, BO all sts. Break yarn, leaving approx 2 yds. Thread this yarn on tapestry needle and work whipstitching around rolled neck edge, spacing every 5 or 6 sts and pulling firmly so neck mimics *T-twist hem*. Weave in rem ends.

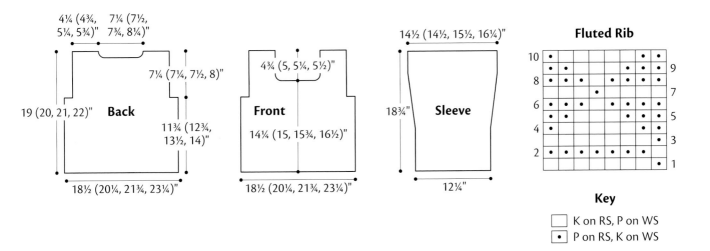

Back

4¼ (4¾, 5¼, 5¾)"   7¼ (7½, 7¾, 8¼)"

7¼ (7¼, 7½, 8)"

19 (20, 21, 22)"

11¾ (12¾, 13½, 14)"

18½ (20¼, 21¾, 23¼)"

Front

4¾ (5, 5¼, 5½)"

14¼ (15, 15¾, 16½)"

18½ (20¼, 21¾, 23¼)"

Sleeve

14½ (14½, 15½, 16¼)"

18¾"

12¼"

Fluted Rib

Key

☐ K on RS, P on WS
⊡ P on RS, K on WS

Abbreviations

alt	alternate(ing)		patt	pattern
approx	approximately		PM	place marker(s)
beg	begin(s)(ning)		rem	remaining
BO	bind off		rep	repeat
CC	contrasting color		rev sc	reverse single crochet
ch	chain		rnd(s)	round(s)
CO	cast on		RS	right side
cont	continue		RT	right twist
dc	double crochet		sc	single crochet
dec	decrease(ing)		SK2P	slip 1 stitch knitwise to right-hand needle, knit 2 stitches together, pass slipped stitch over stitch formed by knitting 2 together and off needle
dpn	double-pointed needle(s)			
foll	follow(s)(ing)			
inc	increase(ing)			
K	knit		sl	slip(ped)
K1f&b	knit into front and back of same stitch		sl st	slip stitch
K2tog	knit 2 stitches together		ssk	slip 2 stitches knitwise one at a time to right-hand needle, knit 2 slipped stitches together through back loops
K3tog tbl	knit 3 stitches together through the back loops			
kwise	knitwise		sskp	slip 2 stitches knitwise one at a time to right-hand needle, knit 1 stitch, pass 2 slipped stitches over knit stitch
MC	main color			
M1L	make 1 stitch left slanting			
M1R	make 1 stitch right slanting		ssp	slip 2 stitches purlwise one at a time to right-hand needle, purl 2 slipped stitches together
meas	measure(s)			
opp	opposite		st(s)	stitch(es)
P	purl		St st	stockinette stitch
P1f&b	purl 1 into front and back of stitch		tbl	through back loop
P2tog	purl 2 stitches together		tog	together
P2tog tbl	purl 2 stitches together through the back loops		WS	wrong side
			YO	yarn over
P3tog	purl 3 stitches together		wyif	with yarn in front

Techniques

If you're unfamiliar with any of the techniques mentioned in the project instructions, you'll find more information about them here.

LONG-TAIL CAST ON

Make a slipknot, leaving a long tail. With the needle held in your right hand, insert the needle into the slipknot. Wrap the nonworking yarn (tail end) around left thumb from front to back and the working yarn (ball end) over right index finger, holding it firmly with other fingers. Wrap the working yarn over the needle as if to knit, pulling the yarn through the loop on thumb to form a stitch. Drop the loop off the needle and tighten by adjusting nonworking yarn.

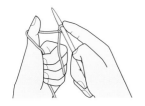

CABLE CAST ON

With the wrong side of work facing and at least two stitches on the left-hand needle, *insert the right-hand needle between the first two stitches on the left-hand needle, yarn over as if to knit, and pull the yarn through, placing the new loop on the left-hand needle (one new stitch cast on). Repeat from * as instructed.

BACKWARD-LOOP CAST ON

Make a slipknot and place it on the needle. *With the needle held in right hand, make a loop around the thumb of left hand. Insert the needle into the loop, tightening it as thumb is slipped out; repeat from * as instructed.

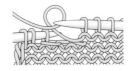
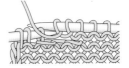

MAKE ONE LEFT (M1L)

Insert the left-hand needle from front to back to lift the strand of yarn between the last stitch knit and the next stitch to be knit. Knit this strand through the back loop. The new stitch slants left.

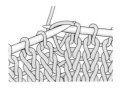

MAKE ONE RIGHT (M1R)

Insert the left-hand needle from back to front to lift the strand of yarn between the last stitch knit and the next stitch to be knit. Knit this strand through the front loop. The new stitch slants right.

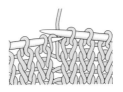

THREE-NEEDLE BIND OFF (3-NEEDLE BO)

Place the stitches from the two pieces to be joined on separate needles. With the right sides together and needles parallel, insert a third needle knitwise into the first stitch on each needle and knit the two stitches together as one. *Knit the next two stitches together in the same manner. With two stitches on the third needle, pass the first stitch

over the second stitch and off the needle. Repeat from *
until all the stitches have been bound off.

 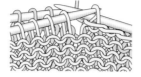

Knit together 1 stitch from front
needle and 1 stitch from back.   Bind off.

HALF-STITCH SEAM ALLOWANCE

When working with a chunky or bulky yarn, taking
a full-stitch seam allowance makes a bulky seam
allowance. Work the seam into the first stitch at each
seam edge instead of between the first and second
stitches at the seam edge.

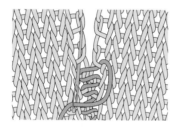

PICKING UP STITCHES

Picking up stitches along a shaped edge is a bit different
than picking up along a bound-off edge. Both are
explained here.

Along Bound-Off Edge

Working from right to left and with the right side facing
(or as instructed), insert the needle into the center of the
stitch below the bound-off edge. Wrap the yarn around
the needle and pull up a loop. Pick up one stitch for every
bound-off stitch unless instructed otherwise.

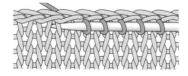

Along Shaped Edge

Working from right to left and with the right side facing
(or as instructed), insert the needle between the purl bars
along a shaped edge. Wrap the yarn around the needle

and pull up a loop. Pick up approximately three stitches
for every four rows, adjusting as needed or as instructed.

WHIPSTITCH

Working from right to left, with a threaded tapestry
needle and the piece(s) facing as instructed, pass
the needle from front to back through the piece(s) to
be stitched. Bring the needle over the piece(s) and pass
the needle through from front to back again slightly to
the left of the previous stitch, pulling firmly to secure.
Repeat as instructed.

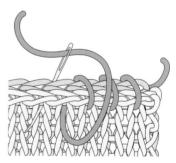

I-CORD

Cast on or slip stitches for I-cord to double-pointed
needles. Knit all the stitches. Do not turn work. *Slide
the stitches to the right-hand end of the needle. Pull
the yarn firmly across the back of work and knit all the
stitches. Repeat from * for desired length.

CROCHET

Several of the projects use one or two crochet techniques for finishing work.

Chain

If no loop is already on the crochet hook, make a slipknot and place it on the hook. *Yarn over the hook and pull up through the loop on the hook, forming a new loop. Repeat from * as instructed.

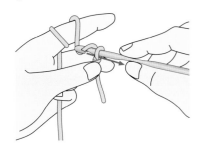

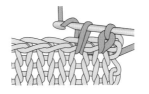
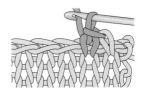

Double Crochet

*Yarn over the hook and insert the hook in the next stitch. Yarn over the hook and pull up the yarn through the stitch (three loops on the hook). Yarn over the hook and pull up the yarn through two loops on the hook (two loops on the hook). Yarn over the hook and pull up the yarn through two loops on the hook (one loop remains on the hook). Repeat from * as instructed.

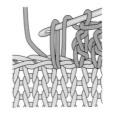

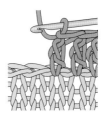

Slip Stitch

Working from right to left, insert the hook into the stitch and pull up a loop (one loop on the hook). *Insert the hook into the next stitch, yarn over the hook, and pull up the yarn through the loop on the hook; repeat from * as instructed.

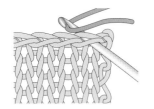
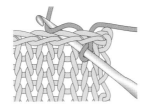

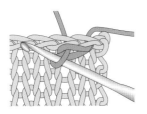

Reverse Single Crochet

Working from *left to right*, insert the hook into the stitch; pull up a loop. Yarn over the hook and pull up the yarn through the loop. *Insert the hook into the next stitch and pull up a loop. Yarn over the hook and pull up through both loops on the hook. Repeat from * as instructed.

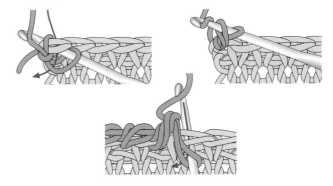

Single Crochet

Working from right to left, insert the hook into the stitch and pull up a loop (one loop on the hook). *Insert the hook into the next stitch, yarn over the hook, and pull up the yarn through the loop on the hook (two loops now on the hook). Yarn over the hook and pull up the yarn through both loops on the hook (one loop on the hook). Repeat from * as instructed.

Useful Information

STANDARD YARN-WEIGHTS							
Yarn-Weight Symbol and Category Name	0 Lace	1 Super Fine	2 Fine	3 Light	4 Medium	5 Bulky	6 Super Bulky
Types of Yarn in Category	Fingering, 10-count crochet thread	Sock, Fingering, Baby	Sport, Baby	DK, Light Worsted	Worsted, Afghan, Aran	Chunky, Craft, Rug	Bulky, Roving
Knit Gauge Range* in Stockinette Stitch to 4"	33 to 40** sts	27 to 32 sts	23 to 26 sts	21 to 24 sts	16 to 20 sts	12 to 15 sts	6 to 11 sts
Recommended Needle in Metric Size Range	1.5 to 2.25 mm	2.25 to 3.25 mm	3.25 to 3.75 mm	3.75 to 4.5 mm	4.5 to 5.5 mm	5.5 to 8 mm	8 mm and larger
Recommended Needle in U.S. Size Range	000 to 1	1 to 3	3 to 5	5 to 7	7 to 9	9 to 11	11 and larger

*These are guidelines only. The above reflect the most commonly used gauges and needle sizes for specific yarn categories.

**Lace-weight yarns are usually knit on larger needles to create lacy, openwork patterns. Accordingly, a gauge range is difficult to determine. Always follow the gauge stated in your pattern.

SKILL LEVELS

Beginner: Projects for first-time knitters using basic knit and purl stitches. Minimal shaping.

Easy: Projects using basic stitches, repetitive stitch patterns, and simple color changes. Simple shaping and finishing.

Intermediate: Projects using a variety of stitches, such as basic cables and lace, simple intarsia, and techniques for double-pointed needles and knitting in the round. Midlevel shaping and finishing.

Experienced: Projects using advanced techniques and stitches, such as short rows, Fair Isle, more intricate intarsia, cables, lace patterns, and numerous color changes.

METRIC CONVERSIONS				
m	=	yds	x	0.9144
yds	=	m	x	1.0936
g	=	oz	x	28.35
oz	=	g	x	0.0352

Resources

Contact the following companies to find shops that carry the fine yarns and buttons used in this book.

YARN

Blue Sky Alpacas
www.blueskyalpacas.com
Bulky Hand Dyes
Skinny Dyed
Suri Merino

Habu Textiles
www.habutextiles.com
A-5 1/5 Kusaki-zome

Knit One, Crochet Too
www.knitonecrochettoo.com
Ambrosia
Brae Tweed
Cotonade
Temptation

LanaKnits
www.lanaknits.com
allhemp3

Mirasol
www.mirasolperu.com
Sulka

Plymouth Yarns
www.plymouthyarn.com
Ashton
King George

Shalimar Yarns
www.shalimaryarns.com
Zoe

Tahki-Stacy Charles
www.tahkistacycharles.com
Zara Plus

Universal Yarns
www.universalyarn.com
Cotton Supreme

BUTTONS

Accessories of Old
www.accessoriesofold.com

Dritz
www.dritz.com

JHB International, Inc.
www.buttons.com

La Mode and La Petite
www.blumenthallansing.com

Bibliography

Epstein, Nicky. *Knitted Embellishments*. Loveland, CO: Interweave Press, 1999.

Epstein, Nicky. *Knitted Flowers*. New York: Sixth & Spring Books, 2006.

Epstein, Nicky. *Knitting on the Edge*. New York: Sixth & Spring Books, 2004.

Parkes, Clara. *The Knitter's Book of Yarn*. New York: Potter Craft, 2006.

Vogue Knitting Magazine Editors. *Vogue Knitting: The Ultimate Knitting Book*. New York: Pantheon, 1989.

Walker, Barbara G. *A Treasury of Knitting Patterns*. Pittsville, WI: Schoolhouse Press, 1998.

Walker, Barbara G. *A Second Treasury of Knitting Patterns*. Pittsville, WI: Schoolhouse Press, 1998.

Wiseman, Nancie. *The Knitter's Book of Finishing Techniques*. Bothell, WA: Martingale & Company, 2002.

YOU MIGHT ALSO ENJOY THESE OTHER FINE TITLES FROM MARTINGALE & COMPANY

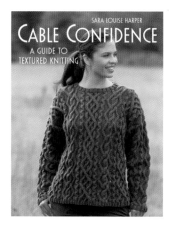

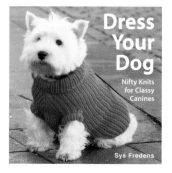

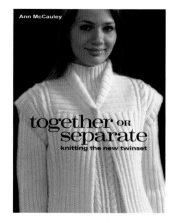

Our books are available at bookstores and your favorite craft, fabric, and yarn retailers.
Visit us at www.martingale-pub.com or contact us at:

1-800-426-3126
International: 1-425-483-3313
Fax: 1-425-486-7596
Email: info@martingale-pub.com

Martingale®
& C O M P A N Y

America's Best-Loved Craft & Hobby Books®
America's Best-Loved Knitting Books®

America's Best-Loved Quilt Books®